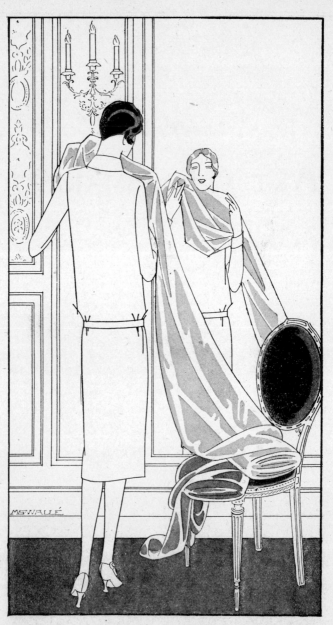

$\mathcal{S}$ELECTING *becoming* COLORS *as they do in* PARIS

The
ART *of* DRESSMAKING

THE BUTTERICK PUBLISHING COMPANY
NEW YORK

Home Dressmaking by Professional Methods

HOWEVER successful a home sewer may be she can usually learn from a professional dressmaker or tailor things that make her work still easier, pleasanter and more effective.

If you are among the number of these successful ones, you will find the following pages filled with just the sort of information you can use profitably.

If you have never tried, or have tried unsuccessfully to make your own clothes, this book offers you the whole story of garment construction from the first elementary stitch to the most effective way of making a tailored pocket or lining a coat.

It is not a book of current styles—those you will find in *Delineator* and the *Butterick Quarterly*—but it has been prepared with the hope that it will be useful and helpful all the time whenever and wherever clothes are being made.

TABLE of CONTENTS

Chapter I

LET YOUR PATTERN WORK FOR YOU

YOUR most dependable assistant in dressmaking is a good pattern, but the amount of service you get from it depends largely upon yourself. When paper patterns were first put upon the market, less than a century ago, they did little for the user except provide cutting outlines of the pieces needed to make a given garment. How these pieces should be put together, how adapted to a figure that differed from the average in any respect, what trimmings were desirable, and what method of finishing was best for that particular garment—all these and other problems were left for the user of the pattern to struggle with.

There is as much difference between these early patterns and the best modern patterns as there is between a wheelbarrow and a high-powered motor-car. This is no disparagement of the wheelbarrow. It is a useful object and, if pushed, will prove helpful; but it can not carry you along by its own power. The only way in which the best modern patterns resemble their remote ancestors is that they provide a cutting outline for each section that must go to the making of the garment; but they provide so much more that the purchaser of one of these patterns who looks upon it only as a cutting guide is failing to make use of its power, just as the owner of a motor-car would be doing if he got out and pushed it. For the motor-car is just as inert as the wheelbarrow until you set the levers and step on the gas. After that it will carry you along to the end of the road.

So the modern pattern will carry you along from the first detail of laying out to the finishing stitch, if you will only set the levers and step on the gas; or, in plainer terms, if you will read and follow the suggestions provided for your service by the manufacturer.

Whether you are an amateur or a professional in the making of garments, the best advice that can be offered is to let your pattern work for you. Experimenting always takes time, even if you are so trained in the art of dressmaking that you can work out your own problems; and the inexperienced dressmaker who depends upon her own ability to create a garment is risking not only this inevitable waste but the destruction of material and even the possibility of ruining her garment entirely.

9

How to Get the Greatest Help from a
Butterick Pattern

1. Decide upon the style you want. (See pages 12 and 13 for suggestions about selecting styles that suit you.)

2. Be measured; then buy the size indicated by the measurements as outlined on pages 13 and 14 unless you vary decidedly from the average in some respect. In that case consult pages 14 and 15 for suggestions as to the size to buy.

3. Look at the views or pictures on the pattern envelope; decide which view represents the design, as you want it, in length of sleeve, etc., and draw a pencil line around it.

4. Read the list of materials suitable for the design printed on the envelope. If the materials are arranged for special views, choose yours from those recommended for the view you have marked. If the materials are not arranged for special views, you may select any one of them.

5. Look at the table of quantities of material required. If the materials are arranged according to views, be sure to select the quantity for your size from the quantities given for the view you have chosen, because if you have selected a long-sleeved view and buy the quantity of material given for a short-sleeved view, you are likely to run short. In such a case you might not be able to match the material, and in any case you would be put to the trouble of going back to the store and the expense of buying the quantity needed for a long sleeve, while if you had purchased the correct amount in the beginning you would have been saved all this trouble and expense. When no quantity is given for a size in a certain width, it means that that size will not cut from that width without ugly piecing or a considerable waste of material.

6. If the quantity of material you intend to buy is likely to be affected by shrinkage, make allowance for this. (See page 242 for approximate amount of shrinkage in various materials.)

7. Measure to see how long your garment should be when finished at the length you prefer. If the length you want your garment to be is greater or less than the length given on the pattern envelope, this should be considered in buying the quantity of material.

8. After making the allowances for shrinkage and for variation of your height from the average, buy the amount of material suggested, in the kind and width suggested.

9. When you get home, open the envelope and take out the pattern and the Deltor.

10. Read the directions on the Deltor for cutting.

11. Spread the Deltor out and select the layout that is meant for the view you have selected, in your size, and for the width and kind of material you have bought; and draw a pencil mark around it. ("Kind of material" means with or without up or down, plaids, stripes, etc.)

12. Open the tissue-paper pattern and identify the pieces by comparing them with the diagram on the back of the envelope. This can be done both by shape and by the numbers printed on the diagram and perforated in the tissue-paper.

13. Select the pieces of pattern that are shown in the layout you have marked on the Deltor; then put the rest back into the envelope, so that you will not cut out any unnecessary parts by mistake.

14. Pin the pattern together and slip it on to see if any adjustments in length are necessary. If so, make them at the places suggested on the Deltor for that particular design. (For general suggestions about lengthening or shortening a pattern, see pages 27-30.)

15. If the material is of a kind that needs to be shrunk, be sure that this has been done.

16. Measure with your tape measure the length and width of the material, to be certain that it is as long and as wide as you think it is.

17. Determine whether there is a right and a wrong side, and if so which is the right side of the material. (See page 58 for suggestions about determining the right and wrong sides of materials.)

18. Lay the pattern pieces on the material exactly as shown in the layout you have marked, pin carefully and cut accurately. (For suggestions about finding the grain of the material, see pages 59-61; for determining the up and down of the material, see page 58; and for the correct methods of pinning and cutting, see page 64.)

19. Read the directions on the Deltor about seams, especially the "Outlet" or "Let-Out" seams, then put together and finish your garment step by step as described and illustrated on the Deltor.

Chapter II

SELECTING YOUR DESIGN AND BUYING
YOUR PATTERN

Becoming Lines—The Correct Size—How to Take Measures

THE ability to select lines that are both becoming and up to date is one of the important preliminaries to being well dressed. There is no unchanging standard by which it is possible to say that one line is always right and another always wrong. Style establishes correctness for the time being, and what is right this year may be wrong next year.

So in order to look well dressed, you must have your clothes accord with the season's lines; but within these limits there is scope for a good deal of variety, and your ability to select the variation that is best suited to your physical characteristics makes it possible for you to have clothes that are becoming as well as smart.

A knowledge of the season's lines is something that must be secured each season, but there are certain principles that are unchanging and that are a help in deciding what versions of the season's lines are best suited to your needs.

Becoming Lines

Take the woman who wants to make herself look smaller, for instance. This problem really has several divisions. There is the woman who is tall and stout, and the woman who is short and stout; there is the woman with large bust and small hips and the woman with a small bust and large hips. On the other side there is the over thin woman who wants to make herself look less thin and the very small woman who would like to look taller. Then there are further details such as cheeks and arms that may be made to look thinner or more rounded, and necks that need to be made to look longer or shorter than they really are.

Correct pattern lines can help tremendously in modifying undesirable outlines, and it will pay you to study your own figure and find out by observing it from all points what general lines are most

12

becoming to you. Then you can make a practise of selecting your patterns from designs that come within these limits.

Lines that will help you to look taller or shorter—If you are very short, whether thin or stout, long unbroken lines running from the top to the bottom of your garment will tend to make you look taller. The same lines are good for the tall, stout figure. If you are too tall, and not stout, select designs with broken lines, such as belts, boleros and yokes, flounces and crosswise tucks or lines of trimming.

Designs that tend to conceal large hips—If you have large hips, avoid a pattern with fulness so arranged that it increases the apparent size of the hips, and avoid equally one that gives the effect of being tighter below the hips than at the hipline, except in certain draped effects where the fulness tends to conceal rather than to accentuate the hips. Laid or stitched lengthwise plaits that give a little spring at the bottom of the skirt, or a circular skirt that fits snugly (but not too snugly) at the hipline, will help to modify the effect of large hips.

Before buying a pattern take time to consider the four essential conditions that will determine its suitability: the age, the height, the weight and the special needs of the person who is to wear the garment. Then having decided on the design you want, be sure to buy the pattern in the correct size.

How to Buy the Right Size of Butterick Patterns

The secret of success in retaining the style and good lines of Butterick Patterns is to buy the correct size—the right size in a pattern means the smallest possible amount of material and no unnecessary alterations. It saves time and money.

Insist on being measured each time you buy a pattern—Butterick Patterns are cut to actual measures of the human figure. Whenever you buy a pattern have your measure taken. Don't rely on your memory or the chance that your figure is the same as it was the last time you bought a pattern. New corsets or a change of diet may have altered your bust, waist or hip measure. Put on your best corsets and a dress that fits nicely. Never have your measure taken over a coat, a clumsy dress, negligée or old corsets. Do not rely on any other pattern or the sizes of ready-made clothes, as they vary with the different manufacturers.

The Necessary Measures

On every Butterick Pattern envelope you will find the measures of the human figure which that pattern was made to fit. These measures are the only ones that are necessary for you to consider in buying the pattern. Do not forget that *the measures are of the figure and not of the pattern.*

For example: a pattern marked 36 bust and 38 hip will fit a figure which measures 36 inches around the bust and 38 inches around the hips. The bust and hip measures of the pattern will be as much more as is necessary to give the correct effect, for the style of the garment, when it is made in the materials for which it is suitable, and to permit the wearer to move about in a normal way and sit down with comfort.

For all garments that are to be worn by the same person—whether dresses, blouses, coats or underwear (except drawers and petticoats)—buy the patterns by the same measures. That is: If you use a 36-bust dress, buy a 36-bust coat and a 36-bust step-in. Don't buy a larger size for your coat, a smaller size for your underwear. The coat patterns make allowance for the dress or waist underneath and the underwear patterns make the proper adjustment in size for being worn under the dress.

Sometimes only the bust measure is given on the pattern envelope. This means that that is the only measure necessary to consider in buying the pattern, and that the style is such that there is sufficient ease or fulness to permit of any reasonable alteration at the waist and hip. If, however, both the bust and hip measures are given, or the bust, waist and hip measures, it means that all the measures given on the envelope must be considered in buying the pattern.

Pattern's for women's skirts, drawers and petticoats should be bought by hip measure. They should never be ordered with a hip measure smaller than that of the figure to be fitted.

Sleeve patterns should be bought by arm measure.

For Large Hips

If your hips are slightly larger than the corresponding measures on the pattern envelope, use the "Outlet" or "Let-Out" seams which Butterick Patterns have at certain edges. (See Illustration 1 on next page.) These seams are wider than the usual three-eighths-inch seam and the sewing line is marked by large round holes referred to on the Deltor as *"large single perforations."* This wider seam is to provide for letting out, if necessary, for figures varying slightly from the average. Any pattern bought by bust size can be "let out" to fit a figure measuring 1½ inch larger around the hips than the list printed on the pattern envelope. (See Illustrations 48 and 49 on page 47.)

If your hips are from two to three and one-half inches larger than the corresponding measures on the pattern envelope, we suggest first finding out if your corset is the type best suited to your figure or if your underwear has too much fulness or is made of too bulky material. We have reduced hips two inches with the correct corsets and underwear.

If the hips really measure from 2 to 3½ inches larger than the corresponding measures on the pattern envelope, we advise buying by the hip measure, taking into consideration the "Outlet" or "Let-Out" seam when buying. Many women of these proportions prefer to buy by their bust size and add on the needed hip size when cutting, because it seems the easier way to them. Certain ways of doing things seem easy to us sometimes because we are familiar with them. This method can be used, but it does not give the best results. On pages 48 and 49 Illustrations 50 and 51 show and the text explains the best way to make the needed alteration. We do not advise buying a pattern of a size more than two inches larger than the bust, lest the neck may be too wide.

If your hip measure is more than three and one-half inches greater than the pattern calls for, you can be fitted more satisfactorily in a garment which has the skirt attached part of the way or all the way around, or with fulness introduced in some way so that it breaks the line of the figure at the hip.

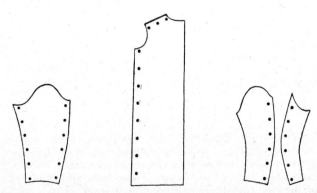

1—A row of large single perforations at shoulder, underarm, or sleeve edge indicates an "Outlet" or "Let-Out" Seam

How to Take Measures

Women's Patterns
(See Illustrations 2 and 3)

Bust—Take the bust measure over the fullest part of the bust, close up under the arms and straight across the back. If the tape is held too high at the back, the measure will be too large; if too low, it will be too small. This measure should always be taken from the back, and the tape should be close, not tight.

Waist—Take the waist measure at your natural waistline, drawing the tape measure close, but not tight.

Hip—Take the hip measure seven inches below the natural waistline. The tape should be close, not tight. This measure should always be taken from the back.

Arm—Take your arm measure easily around the largest part of the arm, about one inch below the armhole.

Young Girls' and Small Women's Patterns
(See Illustrations 2 and 3)

Young girls of the same age vary in size. In addition to the measures, the average age is given on the pattern envelope, to make clear that the pattern is cut on young girls' lines; but the only way to get the correct size is to buy by measures the same as for women.

The measures are taken the same as for women with one exception: the hip measure should be taken around the fullest part of the hip.

Juniors' and Girls' Patterns
(See Illustrations 4 and 5)

Girls of the same age vary in size. In addition to the measures, the average age is given on the pattern envelope to make clear that the pattern is cut on juvenile lines; but the only way to get the correct size is to buy by measures. The bust measure only is needed for patterns of dresses, coats and underwear (except drawers). Drawers should be bought by waist measure.

Bust—Take the bust measure over the bust, close up under the arms and straight across the back. The measure should always be taken from the back and the tape should be easy, not snug.

Waist—Take the waist measure at the natural waistline, drawing the tape measure snug, but not tight.

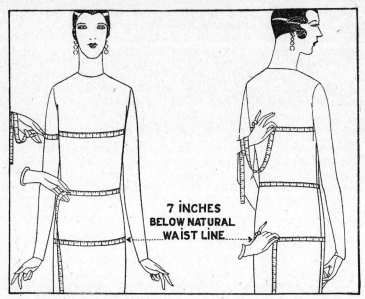

7 INCHES
BELOW NATURAL
WAIST LINE

2—*Measuring waist and arm*   3—*Measuring bust and hips*

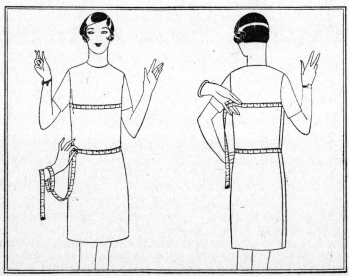

4—*Measuring a girl's waist*   5—*Measuring a girl's bust*

Alteration in length, if necessary, is explained on the Deltor which is enclosed in every Butterick Pattern envelope.

Hats

Hats should be bought by head measure taken around the head as shown in illustration 6. The hat will measure more according to the position in which it is worn on the head.

To Measure Doll

Take the length of the doll from top of head to sole of foot. Take the breast measure as shown in illustration 7. Both of these measures should be considered in buying the pattern, but in general we advise buying by breast measure and altering the length.

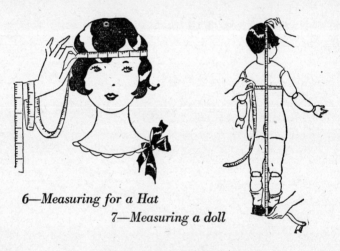

6—Measuring for a Hat

7—Measuring a doll

Men's and Boys' Patterns
(See Illustrations 8, 9, 10 and 11)

Shirts—Buy his shirt patterns by his neck measure, guided either by his collar size, by a comfortable shirt, or by his neck. If you buy the shirt patterns by his collar size, find out whether he prefers the neckbands of his shirts half an inch or a quarter of an inch smaller than his collar, or the same size. It is a matter of individual preference. Either is correct.

If no collar is available, take a shirt that is comfortable, measure it from the center of the buttonhole in the right end of the neckband to the center of the buttonhole in the left end. Or measure his bare neck where the neckband comes. Do it carefully and hold the tape measure easy.   Add half an inch to this measure for the correct shirt size.   This is for ease.

Nightshirts—Buy nightshirt patterns by the same neck measure as you would a regular shirt.   Don't buy a larger size.   The nightshirt pattern is made to fit a man with the neck size marked on the pattern envelope and has the necessary allowance for an easier fit around the neck and through the body.

Butterick shirt patterns allow for all shrinkage in silk and cotton materials.   Woolen materials should be shrunk before cutting.

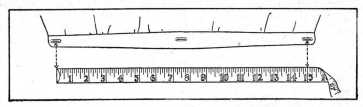

8—*In measuring a collar band be sure that the measure is taken between the centers of the end buttonholes*

9—*The tape measure should be easy, not snug, when the measure for a shirt pattern is taken on the neck*

Men's Patterns

Order patterns for coats, house jackets, bathrobes, smocks, overalls, pajamas and underwear by breast measure; and for trousers and drawers by waist and hip measures.

Boys' Patterns

Boys of the same age vary in size.   In addition to the measures, the average age is given on the pattern envelope of boys' patterns, but the only way to get the correct size is to buy by measures.

Order patterns for his blouses, suits, coats, bathrobes, over-alls, pajamas and underwear by his breast measure; for his trousers and drawers by waist measure.

The measurement for an overcoat should be taken over the clothing the coat is to cover.

How to Take Measures for Men and Boys

Take breast measure around the body close under the arms, drawing the tape snug, but not tight.

Take waist measure at the natural waistline, drawing the tape measure snug, but not tight.

Take hip measure around the fullest part of the hip. The tape should be easy, not snug.

10—Taking breast and   11—Taking the waist
hip measures   measure

Alterations

Alterations for figures varying from the average are illustrated and explained in Chapter IV.

Individual advice will be sent to any one who will explain her dressmaking problems in a letter addressed to Eleanor Chalmers.

Chapter III

SELECTING YOUR MATERIALS

Weaves, Designs, Colors and Qualities

AFTER you have chosen a suitable style and bought the correct size of pattern, the next step in the making of your garment is the selection of the material. This should be suited to the design by which it is to be made, to the purpose to which it is to be put, and to the physical characteristics of the person who is to wear it.

It is important to select it from the list of materials recommended on the pattern envelope, because every Butterick Pattern is designed and made for certain kinds of materials. This is the only way it is possible to have a good effect in a garment, because, as we have pointed out before, if you attempt to make up in heavy wool a dress that is intended to be made of a sheer silk, the result will be unsatisfactory; and the other way around. It is impossible to overemphasize the importance of the question in assuring success in dressmaking.

Choosing Weaves and Designs

The effect of any garment depends very largely on choosing a material that is suitable for the design, considering always the season's mode and the special use to which it is to be put. It is not advisable, for instance, to choose a crisp silk that will give the bouffant effect for a style which is intended to be soft and clinging, or to use a soft, clinging fabric when it is desirable to have the bouffant effect.

Wiry materials may plait well but do not lend themselves to gathers; nap materials do not as a rule tuck well; velvets and other materials that are rich in themselves should be made plainly to bring out the beauty of their texture; it is not a good plan to use plaid for a pattern that is cut into many small pieces, and the same holds true with large figured and bordered materials.

In general it may be given as a safe principle that when the design of the garment is complex the design of the material should be simple. When garments are cut on simple lines, figured materials may be used appropriately.

21

A material that has had a great vogue and that has become passé should never be used for a new dress, for it will give the dress an out-of-date appearance.

In planning the patterns for any season, the Butterick designers keep in constant touch with the manufacturers of textiles. They know far ahead what sort of materials and designs are to be manufactured. They have the materials to work with and every Butterick Pattern is designed to be made up not only in certain types of fabrics but in fabrics that are in harmony with the style trend of the season.

Selecting Colors to Bring Out Your Best Points

Everybody has best points, and color plays a large part in bringing them out, as well as subduing undesirable characteristics. Beautiful eyes may be made more beautiful and nondescript eyes may be given a glint the owner never dreamed they possessed if she will choose just the right color and just the right shade or tone of that color. Because tones and shades are most important. A blue too brilliant may make eyes look colorless where a softer tone would give them added blueness.

It is never safe to buy a color to wear just because you happen to like it. The ability to select becoming colors is something that requires a trained eye, and the only way to train the eye for this purpose is by using it to look at colors in connection with the person who is to wear them.

Probably most of us have friends who are always choosing the wrong color—the florid-skinned woman with a passion for too vivid pink; the fragile, blue-veined blonde who can not resist just the shade of blue that makes her look entirely washed out, and the woman with bright red hair who yearns for scarlet or magenta.

There are certain general principles that are a help as a starting-point in selecting becoming colors, which must be chosen to accord with

The color of your hair
The color of your eyes
The color of your skin

Size must not be overlooked. For the woman who has too much size it is well to remember that dark colors tend to make you look smaller, but it is a mistake to feel that if you are large you must confine yourself entirely to dark colors. It is possible for the woman of well-developed figure to escape from the everlasting round of black, dark blue, dark green, dark brown and dark gray if she will keep two cautions in mind:

Choose neutral shades instead of vivid ones.
Chose dull-surfaced fabrics of inconspicuous designs and avoid shiny materials with sharply outlined figures.

The following suggestions will serve as a starting-point in selecting the colors that are becoming, but in a world where there are millions of people and no two absolutely alike it is easy to see that no chart can take the place of the trained eye, and no better way of selecting colors has ever been devised than the method followed in the ateliers of the great Paris couturiers.

Here the customer stands before a full-length mirror and drapes the end of a bolt of material around her face. The saleswoman stands near her. In this way both the saleswoman and the customer can study the effect and decide whether the shade is becoming or unbecoming. (See Frontispiece.)

It is not necessary to have a full-length mirror or a trained attendant to do this. Any woman standing in front of any looking-glass can try various colors against her own face and learn, by comparing them, which ones bring out the best points in her skin, hair and eyes.

Some Suggestions for Selecting Colors

The following suggestions are based on the natural tones of complexion, hair and eyes. Where make-up is used it modifies the combination and must of course be taken into consideration in selecting colors for garments.

As a general rule:

If your hair is dark, choose rich, warm colors.

If you are blond haired, choose delicate clear colors.

If you are auburn or red haired, choose pure greens, slightly grayed, and warm shades of blue and brown.

If you are gray or white haired, choose from the varieties of blue, purple or green, except yellowish green. Wine, soft shades of rose, black and white combinations are very good. Usually the soft silvery tones of any color are most becoming. If a gray-haired woman has plenty of color in the face, gray should be becoming. The gray should match or blend with the hair.

To these general suggestions may be added some further details.   For instance:

The girl with golden hair, fair skin and blue eyes will find generally that the following are good colors:
>   Black, which makes an effective contrast
>   Mauve, because it enhances her coloring
>   Nile green, which, being complementary to red, emphasizes her coloring, but, like mauve, is delicate enough to suit her type
>   Soft blues, of course—but everybody knows that!

For a girl of this type the following are generally to be avoided:
>   Emerald green and royal blue, because they are too strong
>   Mulberry, which is too heavy for one with cool coloring.

The medium-light blonde with rather sallow skin and gray eyes will as a rule find her best colors among the following:
>   Orchid and rose pink, because they reflect their color in her face
>   Navy blue, which by contrast gives character to her hair and skin
>   Cream and ivory, which tend to make the skin look white.

She will do well generally to avoid such colors as:
>   Copenhagen blue, because it brings out sallowness of skin
>   Dead white, which by contrast makes the skin more sallow
>   Putty and sand shades, which are too much like her own coloring and add no character to the costume.

The medium blonde with fair skin and high coloring and with hazel eyes usually looks her best in such colors as:
>   Lip-stick red, which lessens high color and enhances the fairness of the skin
>   Apricot, which though delicate brings out the natural color
>   Lanvin green, a cool color which enhances the coloring of the skin and eyes.

She should be careful about such colors as:
>   Lemon, which is too pale and characterless
>   Olive, a heavy shade which is too nearly the color of her hair and reflects unbecoming green in the skin
>   Alice blue, because it is too light and brings out the yellow in her skin.

The woman with dark-brown hair and eyes, vivid coloring and dark skin can generally wear successfully:
> Buff, which by contrast is often becoming to one with warm coloring
> Orange or geranium red, because these lessen the natural color.

Poor colors for her type are:
> Chocolate brown, which produces an uninteresting one-color effect
> Electric blue, because bright blue brings out the yellow in the skin
> Mauve, which is too delicate for the strong type.

The auburn or red haired woman with brown eyes and delicate coloring will find the following are usually good colors for her type:
> White, which forms a striking contrast with the hair
> Golden brown, a becoming shade bringing out the glints in the hair
> Bishop purple, a strong color suitable for her type.

Shades that she will generally do well to avoid are:
> Lemon yellow, which is too delicate and gives a yellowish cast to the skin
> Copper or red shades that do not harmonize with the hair
> Soft green, which enhances an already dominant color.

The large woman of medium coloring will find that the following colors are usually becoming:
> Midnight blue, which is inconspicuous and therefore good for the large figure
> Beaver, a rich color but inconspicuous
> Bottle green, which enhances coloring and affords relief from ordinary dark shades
> Eggplant (purple), especially good in Georgette and similar soft fabrics
> Neutral and not too pale shades of blue, taupe and smoky gray.

Colors to be avoided by the woman of large proportions are:
> Flesh, silver gray, tangerine and similar conspicuous colors that tend to make the figure appear larger than it really is.

Colors for Evening

It must be kept in mind in selecting materials for evening garments that artificial light affects the becomingness of colors. Always try the material for an evening dress against your face under artificial light.

Fashion in Color

There is fashion in color as well as in design and material. Each season there are new colors or new shades of familiar colors. These are offered in variety to suit all types of faces. One has simply to choose one's own best colors from those shown.

The colored illustrations in the magazines are a help in selecting seasonable and appropriate colors. The colors and materials illustrated are the newest. Note those that are used in garments for young girls and for women of various ages. You will see that young girls wear more color than grown-ups, and the younger the girl the daintier the color. Youth calls for variety in color. Maturity requires dignified and harmonious color combinations. Bright colors are in good taste for older women for sports and evening and summer dresses, and it is better on the whole to err on the side of bright and cheerful colors than to fall into the habit of wearing drab and uninteresting shades at all times.

Quality in Materials

The judging of quality in textiles is a highly specialized business that requires long study and a wide experience, and the safest course for the average buyer to follow is to trade with a reliable merchant and depend upon him to sell only materials that are as represented. Moreover, many of the large manufacturers are now marking their fabrics at intervals on the selvage, and materials so marked of course usually carry the manufacturer's own guarantee.

If you want an all-linen or an all-wool or an all-silk material, tell your merchant so and depend upon him to sell you what you ask for. It seems timely to mention, however, that modern methods of textile manufacture are producing very satisfactory results from a great variety of mixtures, and you may cut yourself off from many beautiful as well as durable and inexpensive fabrics if you base your requirements in the purchase of materials too rigidly on standards that formerly prevailed.

Chapter IV

ALTERATIONS FOR FIGURES THAT VARY FROM THE AVERAGE

Alterations That Must Be Made in the Pattern Before Cutting Out the Garment—Alterations That Can Be Made in the Garment After It Is Cut

BUTTERICK Patterns are fitted on human figures of average proportions. But a woman may measure exactly 36 inches around the bust, and have the correct hip measure, and yet be longer or shorter waisted, or have a longer or shorter arm, or the upper part of her arm may be long in proportion to the lower part, or vice versa, thus bringing the elbow of the pattern in the wrong place, or she may be longer or shorter from the natural waistline to the floor.

Alterations That Must Be Made in the Pattern Before the Garment Is Cut

Alterations in Length

The variation in any one place may not be marked enough to be noticeable, but, *before cutting your material*, any necessary changes in length should be made in the pattern. This will make the pattern the right length for your particular figure and save unnecessary alterations after the garment is cut. The alterations are very easy to make and the pattern is planned so that they can be done without altering the original lines of the pattern. By making the changes when necessary, however, you will give the garment the unmistakable look of having been made for you.

In some cases, such as in a straight one-piece dress, all alterations in length can be made at the bottom; but in most cases, especially where there are cross-lines, such as an attached skirt, cross-dart at the hip, lines for trimming, set-in pockets, etc., the alteration should be divided—part of it made above the natural waistline and part below—in order to retain the original lines and proportions of the pattern.

It is best always to follow the instructions given in the Deltor enclosed in the envelope of the pattern you are using as to the best place to make the alteration in length of that particular pattern.

27

The Best Way to Test the Length of a Pattern

The most direct and easily understood way to find out how much change is necessary in the length of a pattern is to pin the front and back together, leaving the underarm seams open about six inches below the armhole.

If there is an attached skirt or band which forms part of the length, pin it on, or if the pattern has a hem, turn it up.

Pin the top of the sleeve to the armhole, and if the sleeve has a cuff or wristband which forms part of the length, pin it in place. Be careful to pin seams and hems the exact width allowed on the pattern.

Take off your dress and pin a tape measure around your figure over your underwear and at your natural waistline. The tape should be snug enough to stay in place but not tight enough to slip up.

Have some one help you to slip the pattern on over your underwear, being very careful to have the neck and center front and center back in correct position on your figure. Place the small double perforations in the front of the pattern (indicating the natural waistline) at the lower edge of the tape measure. (Illustrations 12-15.)

If there is too much length above these perforations, pin a tuck or plait across the front to show how much. (Illustrations 12 and 13.) Decide how far from the floor you want the garment to be. The length varies with the fashion. If the pattern is too long, make the alteration at the place suggested in the Deltor of the pattern you are using. Do not make your calculations too closely; it is best to allow about an inch for the give and take of making.

If you are long-waisted and tall instead of short, the pattern can be altered at the same points by cutting across the pattern pieces and separating them sufficiently to give you the length needed, pinning a piece of paper under each slash to hold the pieces in position. (Illustrations 14 and 15.)

Have the sleeve edges pinned together at the wrist. If the sleeve pattern has perforations or gathers at the elbow, use your free hand to hold this point at your elbow with the arm bent.

If the sleeve is full length, it must be long enough to reach from your shoulder along the outside of your arm to the wrist with your arm bent. This is for a plain sleeve or a soft, tailored sleeve. (Illustrations 13 and 14.)

A sleeve bloused at the wrist will need enough length to give as soft an effect as desired. (Illustrations 12 and 15.)

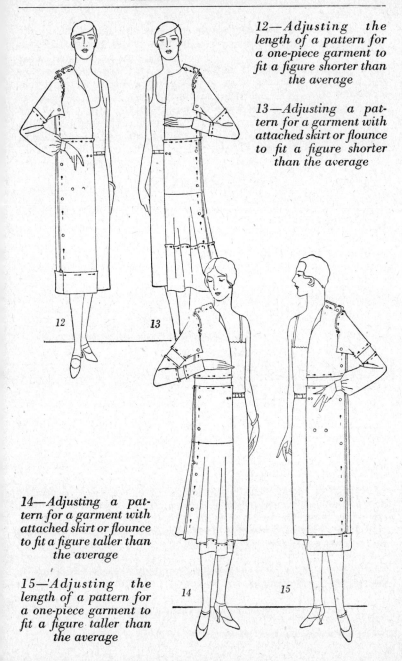

12—*Adjusting the length of a pattern for a one-piece garment to fit a figure shorter than the average*

13—*Adjusting a pattern for a garment with attached skirt or flounce to fit a figure shorter than the average*

14—*Adjusting a pattern for a garment with attached skirt or flounce to fit a figure taller than the average*

15—*Adjusting the length of a pattern for a one-piece garment to fit a figure taller than the average*

If the sleeve is too long above or below the elbow or in both places, have a plait pinned in to show how much, having it pinned in the place suggested in the Deltor of the pattern you are using. If the sleeve is too short, have it cut across and a piece or pieces pinned in, to show how much it needs lengthening.

This trying on of the pattern is not for any other adjustment but to decide on any necessary change of length.

Take the pattern off, unpin the seams and smooth out the pieces, as you can alter the pattern better when the pieces are flat; but be sure to work very carefully.

To Shorten the Pattern

Make the plait the same width all the way across each of the pieces shortened.

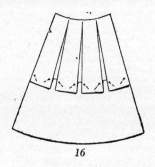

16—The correct way to shorten a pattern for a circular lower part less than three yards wide

16

In shortening a circular lower part less than 3 yards wide, slash the pattern about where the plait is pinned, slashing an equal distance from the lower edge all the way across, and lap the upper portion over the lower the amount pinned in the plait. Slash the upper portion in three or four places, evenly spaced, to within $\frac{3}{8}$ of an inch of the top and separate the pieces an equal amount to make it fit the lower portion, being careful to lap the upper part over the lower the same amount all the way across. (Illustration 16.) This will keep the lower edge width and the ripples will fall as they did in the original model.

A circular lower part measuring more than 3 yards wide may be shortened at the bottom.

To Lengthen the Pattern

Separate the pattern pieces an even width all the way across.

Miscellaneous Alterations That Must Be Made
Before Cutting

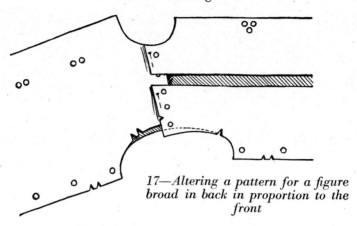

17—Altering a pattern for a figure broad in back in proportion to the front

Altering a Pattern for a Figure Broad in Back in Proportion to the Front

USUALLY this type of woman is hollow-chested. The alteration for this type of figure is very simple, but it must be done in the pattern before cutting the material.

Slash the back pattern from the shoulder to the bottom on a line with the back edge and separate the pieces as much as is necessary to fit the figure. (Illustration 17.) This will make the shoulder of the back longer than the shoulder of the front. (Illustration 30.)

Half of this difference in width should be sloped off the armhole edge of the back. (Illustration 17.) Half the difference should be filled in at the armhole of the front, letting the allowance slope to nothing at the notches. The dotted line in Illustration 17 shows you where to fill in and where to slope off.

Altering Skirt Patterns for a Prominent Abdomen

If a woman has a slightly rounded or a decidedly prominent abdomen, an alteration is necessary to give her extra length at the top. If this alteration is not made in cutting, the skirt will draw up in front and stand out in an ugly manner. (Illustration 18.) The amount of the alteration will depend on the prominence of the abdomen. It may be necessary to add from ½ inch to 1½ inch to the skirt at the center front, letting the allowance slope to nothing at the side. A skirt should fall in a straight line from the fullest part of the abdomen to the bottom.

18—*This skirt is cut to allow for a prominent abdomen but is basted on the normal pattern lines*

19

20—*The extra material dropped at the top and let out at the sides makes the skirt hang correctly*

19—*Cutting a skirt to fit a prominent abdomen. The shaded part represents the material allowed beyond the pattern line*

Illustration 19 shows the alteration that is necessary in a skirt pattern with two or more pieces. The front of the skirt must be extended at the top when cutting, this extension gradually decreasing to nothing at the side.

In extending the front the waistline becomes smaller, so the side edge of the piece must be increased to keep the waistline the original size. This extension at the side should slope to nothing at the hipline. Mark the outline of the edge of the pattern with bastings.

Cut out the skirt, baste it together and baste it to the belt, following the instructions in the Deltor of the pattern you are using.

Slip the skirt on, being careful to place the top in exactly the right place around the figure. Then rip the skirt from the belt across the front and down the side seams to the hipline and let it drop at the top as much as necessary to make it hang in a straight line below the abdomen. Let out the side edge as much as necessary to give the needed waist size. (Illustration 20.)

In extending the top of a circular skirt when cutting, you make the waistline smaller so if the waistline was the correct size for you in the first place, it will be necessary to increase the size of the new waistline to keep it the original size of the pattern.

This can be done by lifting the skirt all around a trifle. In extreme cases, it may be necessary to lift the skirt enough so that it will be necessary to put a dart at the center front to make it fit the belt, but usually a slight easing into the belt at the front will be sufficient.

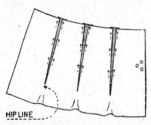

21—A circular yoke pattern slashed to fit a waist larger than the average

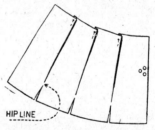

22—Plaits laid in circular yoke pattern to fit a waist smaller than the average

If your waist is large or small in proportion to your hips, it will be necessary to alter the waist size of a circular yoke pattern. The alteration is very simple.

If the waist size is too small for you, slash the yoke pattern from the upper edge to the hipline, making the slashes in three places.

In laying the yoke pattern on your material, spread the upper edge until it is the right size for you.   (Illustration 21.)

If the waistline is too large for you, make three dart-shaped plaits in the yoke pattern, laying the plaits in the upper edge, and letting them taper to nothing at the hipline.   (Illustration 22.)   The depth of the plaits depends on the amount of alteration required.

Altering a Sleeve Pattern for a Very Large Arm

If the arm is large at the elbow as well as above, slash from top to bottom and separate the pieces as much as needed.   (Illustration 23.)   If the arm is large above the elbow and not at the elbow, slash from top to elbow and across at elbow and separate the pieces as much as needed.   (Illustration 24.)

The armhole will probably be too small—slash it until it feels just right, being careful not to overlook the fact that ⅜ inch must be taken off for a seam.

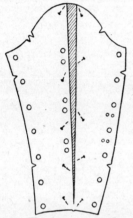

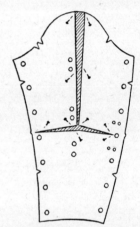

23—To fit an arm large at the elbows, as well as above

24—To fit an arm large above but not at the elbow

Alterations That Can Be Made in the Garment After It Is Cut

Alterations to fit the following variations can be made in the garment after it is cut and basted.   In basting, follow carefully the instructions given in the Deltor enclosed in the envelope of the pattern you are using.

Try the garment on.   It is of course a great advantage to have some one help you, but if you are alone you can manage very nicely by standing in front of a mirror.

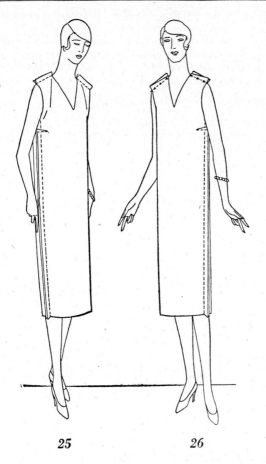

25   26

Altering Garments to Fit Sloping Shoulders

Sloping shoulders make a diagonal wrinkle from the neck toward the armhole. (Illustrations 25 and 27.) The wrinkle is due to the fact that the shoulders are not high enough to take up the full size of the pattern.

If the garment has an open neck and the wrinkle is very slight—more of a slight pull than a wrinkle (Illustration 25)—the shoulder edge of the front can be dropped a little at the neck, tapering this off to nothing at the armhole. (Illustration 26.) The "Outlet" or "Let-Out" seam provided on the Butterick Patterns makes this alteration possible.

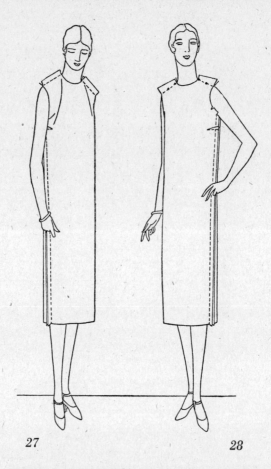

27   28

If the neck is to be worn high or the wrinkle is very pronounced (Illustration 27), the extra size must be taken up at the shoulder seams. Take up as much as necessary at the armhole, tapering this amount off to nothing at the neck. (Illustration 28.)

Taking in the shoulder seams will decrease the size of the atmhole and make it bind. Slash the armhole a little until it feels just right. Do not slash it too much, or your armhole will be too large after taking off the seam for sewing in the sleeve.

Take off the garment, baste the shoulder seams and cut out the armhole on a line with the slashes. Try the garment on again to be sure that it is comfortable and then stitch the shoulder seams.

Diagonal wrinkles in the back may be handled in the same way.

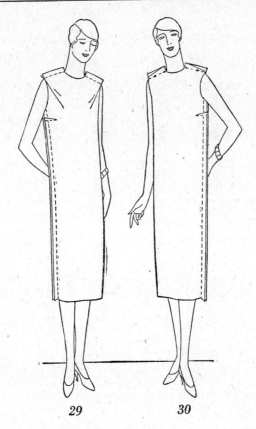

29   30

Altering Garments to Fit Square Shoulders

If the wrinkle is very slight (Illustration 29)—more of a draw
than a wrinkle—due rather to a prominent shoulder bone, the
shoulder edge of the front can be dropped a little at the armhole,
tapering this off to nothing at the neck. The "Outlet" or "Let-
Out" seams on Butterick Patterns make this alteration possible.
(Illustration 30.)

This will increase the size of the armhole and, if the sleeve is
plain at the top, you will need to let out the "Outlet" seam of the
sleeve enough to equal the amount dropped at the shoulder—that
is, let out half the amount on each side of the seam. In basting in
the sleeve, place the notches in the sleeve enough higher than the
corresponding notches in the armhole at front and back to equal
in each place half the total amount dropped at the shoulder so as
to keep the original balance of the sleeve.

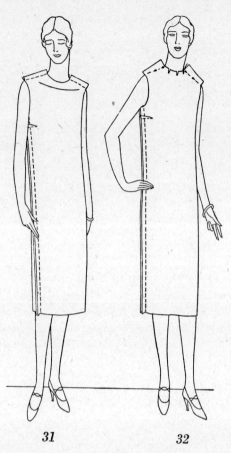

31   32

Illustration 31 shows how a garment will draw across the chest on a square-shouldered figure. It needs to be taken up on the shoulder seams at the neck as much as necessary to remove the wrinkles, letting this alteration slope to nothing at the armhole. Taking in the shoulder seams at the neck will make the neck size too small if the neck is high. Slash the neck edge at intervals until it feels comfortable (Illustration 32), but not so deep that the neck will be too large after taking off the seam for sewing on the collar. Take off the garment and baste the shoulder seams and trim off the neck edge on a line with the slashes. Try on again to be sure the altera- tion is right before stitching the shoulder seams. If there are crosswise wrinkles at the back, the back can be altered in the same way.

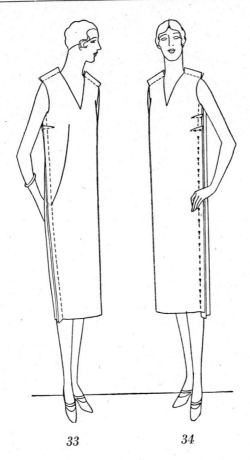

33   *34*

Altering Garments to Fit an Unusually Large Bust

This is the case not necessarily of a large figure but of a figure in which the bust is large in proportion to the rest of the figure. A woman may measure 36 inches at the bust and yet have a narrow back and a very full bust.

The garment will draw in wrinkles that run from the bust downward toward the underarm seam and it will pull up and stand out in front. (Illustration 33.) To remedy this, rip the underarm seam up to within a few inches of the armhole and take up a small dart at the underarm edge of the front, tapering the dart off to nothing at the side of the bust—it can run as far forward as possible without having the end of it show from the front. (Illustration 34.)

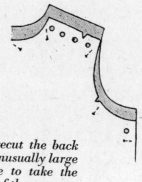

*35—The pattern laid on to recut the back
of a garment adjusted to an unusually large
bust, when it is not desirable to take the
excess length from the bottom of the garment*

The garment may already have a dart at the underarm—if so, it distributes the dart fulness better to take up another dart than to make the first one deeper. To make the most perfect fit for the bust, the end of the dart, if there is only one, should come in line with the fullest part of the bust.

If there are two darts, one should come out just above and the other just below the fullest part of the bust. To get this, you may have to raise or lower the first dart. The size of the new dart should be just enough to make the front of the garment hang in a straight line below the bust.

If the garment already has two darts, take in both darts equally, enough to give the desired effect.

The same amount that is taken up in the new dart will have to be taken off the back. In some cases, such as in a straight one-piece dress, this can be done at the bottom, but when there is an attached skirt or lines for trimming, etc., it is best to take it off the top. To do this, lay the pattern on as shown in Illustration 35 and recut the upper part of the back. Note that the neck, shoulder and armhole edges are placed as much lower than they were cut originally as the amount you took up in the dart. Rebaste the shoulder and underarm seams and try on the garment to be sure it is just right. This dart alteration can also be made in a pattern which has a shoulder dart.

After you have tried this on one garment and found out just the amount necessary to take up in the dart, you can the next time, *before cutting your material*, take the length out of the back by laying a plait across the back in line with the dart.

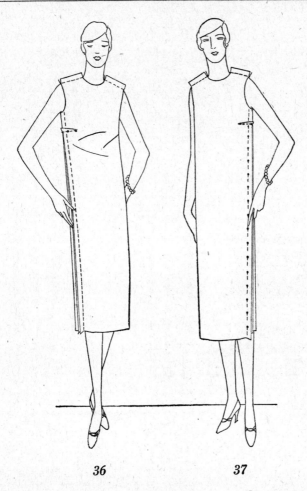

36   37

Altering Garments to Fit an Unusually Small Bust

The garment will show too much length at the center front through the bust and will hug in toward the bottom. (Illustrations 36, 39 and 41.)

For a garment having a dart at underarm seam—If made of plain material, rip the seam and let out the dart as much as necessary to allow the garment to fall straight below the bust. (Illustration 37.) This will make the front longer than the back at the seam. The extra length can be taken off the bottom.

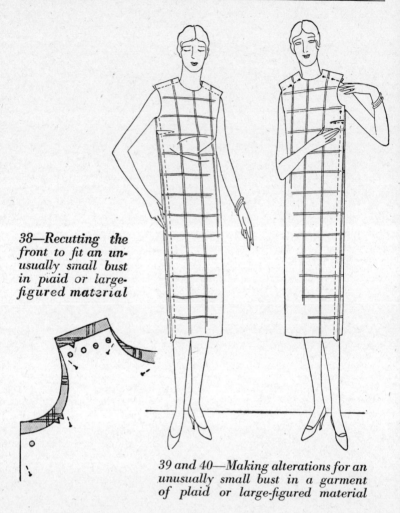

*38—Recutting the
front to fit an un-
usually small bust
in plaid or large-
figured material*

*39 and 40—Making alterations for an
unusually small bust in a garment
of plaid or large-figured material*

If made of plaid, crosswise stripes or material with large figures
which should match at the underarm seam (Illustration 39), the
amount let out of the darts should be pinned up on the shoulder
of the front so that the underarm seam will not be disturbed.
(Illustration 40.)   After finding out just how much needs to be
taken off, lay the pattern on as shown in Illustration 38 and recut
the upper part of the front.   Note that the neck, shoulder and armhole edges are placed as much lower than they were cut originally
as the amount you let out the dart.

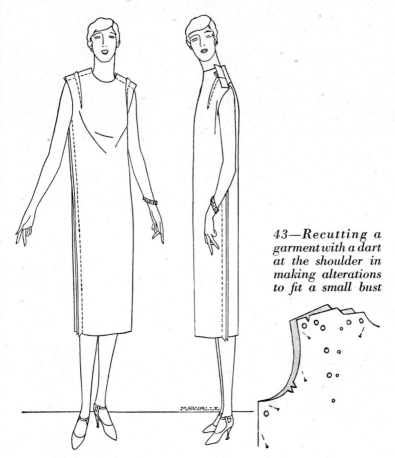

43—*Recutting a garment with a dart at the shoulder in making alterations to fit a small bust*

41 and 42—Making alterations to fit an unusually small bust in a garment that has darts at the shoulders

For a garment having a shoulder dart (Illustration 41), let out the dart as much as necessary on the armhole side, so that there is no change in the line or direction of it. (Illustration 42.) This will make the shoulder too long and you will have to lay your pattern on and recut the armhole, taking off the amount let out. The front will be too long from the shoulder to the bottom of the armhole. After finding out just how much by pinning up the shoulder of the front, lay the pattern on as shown in Illustration 43 and recut the shoulder and neck edges.

44   45

Altering Garments for an Over-Erect Figure

On an over-erect figure, the garment will show wrinkles at the upper part of the back, indicating too much length in the upper part of the garment. (Illustration 44.) Take up the shoulder edge of the back at the neck, tapering it to nothing at the armhole. (Illustration 45.) This will make the neck too high. Slash the neck edge at intervals until it feels comfortable, but do not slash so deep that the neck will be too large after taking off the seam for sewing on the collar. (Illustration 45.) Take off the garment, baste the shoulder seam and trim off the neck edge on a line with the slashes. Try it on again before stitching the shoulder seams.

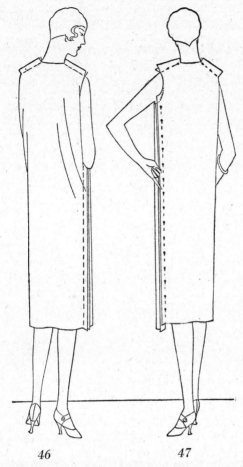

46   47

Altering Garments for a Round-Shouldered Figure

Round shoulders will cause the garment to run in wrinkles from shoulder-blades to underarm seams and lift or draw up across the back. (Illustration 46.) Rip the underarm seam and take up the shoulder edge of the back at the armhole enough to make it hang straight. The amount taken up should be tapered off to nothing at the neck. Ease the shoulder edge of the back to the front as much as you can without having it show. (Illustration 47.) Rebaste the underarm seam with the side edge of the back as much higher than the side edge of the front at the armhole as the shoulder was raised. Trim off the unevenness at the armhole, tapering it off to nothing at the notch in the back as indicated by the dotted line in illustration 47, so that the back will not be made any narrower.

This will make the front longer than the back at the seam. If of plain material, the extra length can be taken off at the bottom. If of plaid, crosswise stripes or material with large figures which should match at the underarm seam, take the length off the top the same as for an "Unusually Small Bust," page 42.

Slight Alterations in Skirts, Drawers and Petticoats

If they are plain at the top, any alterations needed for a waist slightly larger or smaller than the average may be made at the seams or darts or at both.

If the waist is too large, stitch the darts and seams a trifle deeper than the normal seam allowance.

If the waist is too small, they can be let out at the darts or at the seams if a slight allowance is made for the necessary waist size when cutting out your garment. If no allowance is made for this alteration, the garment could be raised a trifle higher on the belt all the way around.

In altering the seams, the alterations should run gradually to the hip, unless the garment is large or small at that point, in which case the alteration should run all the way to the bottom. Be careful not to fit the garment too tightly over the hips or it will draw up and wrinkle when you sit down and will get out of shape. If the garment sets properly, the center line at the front will be perpendicular.

In a circular garment with one or more darts, the waist size can be made smaller or larger by taking in or letting out the darts. In a circular garment without darts, if only a small reduction is required, it may often be eased into the belt.

If the waist needs to be made very much smaller, it may be necessary to make a small dart at each hip.

If the waistline needs to be made larger, it can be done by raising the garment a trifle on the belt all the way around. A very little will increase the waist size a good deal.

If a plaited garment is too large or too small at the waist, the plaits should be made either deeper or shallower to fit the belt.

If the garment is gathered at the top, the gathers simply need to be drawn a little closer or let out as much as needed.

If the garment is made with a yoke, the alterations for a waist larger or smaller than the average should be made in the pattern before cutting out your garment. Directions for making these alterations are given on pages 33 and 34.

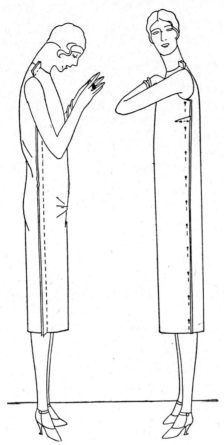

*48 and 49—A garment can be fitted to hips
slightly larger than the average by letting out
the "Outlet" or "Let-Out" seams*

Altering Garments for Hips That Are Slightly
Larger Than the Average

Butterick Patterns have at certain edges what we call "Outlet"
or "Let-Out" seams. These seams are wider than the usual ⅜ inch
and the basting line is marked with large round holes referred to
as "large single perforations." These wide seams provide for letting out the hips ⅜ inch on each side of each seam, making a total
of 1½ inch on the entire garment. (Illustrations 48 and 49.)

Making Alterations in a One-Piece Garment for Hips That Are Decidedly Larger Than the Average

When hips are from two to three and one-half inches larger than the corresponding measures on the pattern envelope it is best to buy a pattern by hip measure and make the necessary alterations.

A figure of these proportions will look best in a dress as easy across the shoulders and bust as it is possible for her to wear without having it look too large. The easy fitting upper part will balance the width of the hips and make them look smaller.

This is a matter of effect and can better be judged by looking at the dress when on the figure (as they do in Paris) than by measures.

It is really wonderful what can be accomplished by the use of correct lines. Having bought the pattern by the hip measure and carefully followed the Deltor in cutting and basting together, slip it on and take a good look at yourself in the mirror. (See Illustration 50 on the opposite page.)

Carefully study both front and back, especially the back, as a narrow back will increase the effect of width in your hips. For the usual set-in sleeve, the joining of the sleeve to the body should come at the turn or round of your shoulders. Stick a pin where you feel the joining of the sleeve to the body should come, leaving the shoulder as long as is becoming without making the garment look too large for you. If the shoulder is too long and the bust too large, take the garment off, rip the shoulder and side seams down as far as the hips and lay the pattern on as shown in Illustration 51, being careful not to overlook the seam for sewing in the sleeve. Take off the shoulder, armhole and underarm edges as indicated in the illustration, tapering the amount off gradually to nothing at the hipline. Note that the pattern will touch the original armhole under the arm.

For the first time, and until you gain confidence in your ability to follow this "professional" method, mark the new line for the armhole and underarm seam with basting thread, but do not cut away the excess material. Rebaste the seams along the new line, baste in the sleeves and try on the garment to be sure it is just right for you. Then cut away the extra material at the armhole along the line of bastings.

Altering a Circular Skirt to Fit Prominent Hips

The skirt will stand out at both sides. Lift the skirt a trifle across the back and across the front if needed, tapering off the amount lifted to nothing over the fullest part of the hips. If this makes the waist size too large, take up a small dart at the hip.

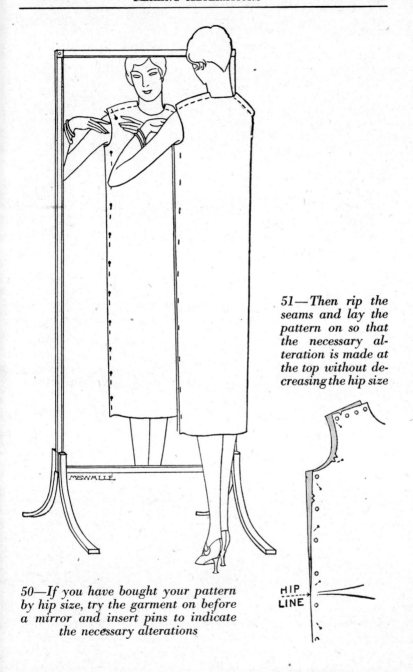

51—Then rip the seams and lay the pattern on so that the necessary alteration is made at the top without decreasing the hip size

HIP LINE

50—If you have bought your pattern by hip size, try the garment on before a mirror and insert pins to indicate the necessary alterations

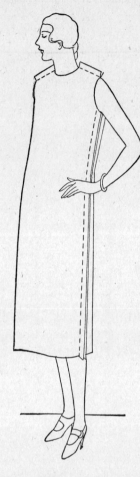

52—When the abdomen is prominent, the lower edge of a garment cut for the average figure will poke out in front unless the necessary alteration is made to correct the line

Altering Garments for a Prominent Abdomen

Alterations for a prominent abdomen in a one-piece garment— The garment will stand out at the front.   (Illustration 52.)

For a one-piece garment with no dart across the hip, rip the underarm seam from the bottom up to the hipline (7 inches below the natural waistline) and take up a dart at the underarm edge of the front large enough to make the garment hang straight below the abdomen.

Taper this dart off gradually to nothing at the side of the abdomen (Illustration 53 on next page), being careful it does not "pout."   Rebaste the seam and try on the garment again to be

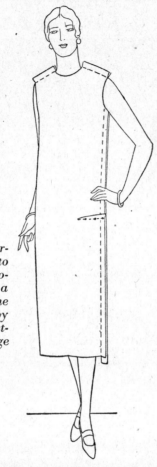

53—A one-piece garment may be fitted to a prominent abdomen by taking a dart at the hip in the front section, or by deepening an existing dart at the edge

sure it is all right. This will make the back longer than the front but this can be taken off at the bottom. (Illustration 53.) The dart can be covered with trimming or a belt.

If the one-piece garment already has a dart across the hip, rip the underarm seam and make the dart enough deeper at the underarm edge of the front to make the garment hang straight below the abdomen. Take this extra amount in on the lower side of the dart in order to keep the line of the dart the same as it was originally.

After you have tried this on one garment and found out just the amount necessary to take up in the dart, you can, the next time, *before cutting your material*, take the length out of the back by laying a plait across the pattern of the back in line with the dart.

54   55

Alteration for a prominent abdomen in a garment with attached skirt. (Illustration 54.) If the skirt is attached about at the hip-line, take up a tuck or plait at the underarm seam just above the seam that joins the skirt to the body. (Illustration 55.) This plait should be deep enough to make the garment hang straight from the abdomen to the bottom. It should be pinned all the way across the back and should taper from the underarm seam to nothing at the side of the abdomen. When the garment hangs just right, take it off and baste the skirt as much higher than it was as the amount pinned up in the plait, but do not cut this amount off until you have tried it on again to make sure that it hangs just right with the seam in a good line around the body. If the skirt is attached at or near the knees, the alteration should be made in the same way as for a one-piece dress, pages 50 and 51.

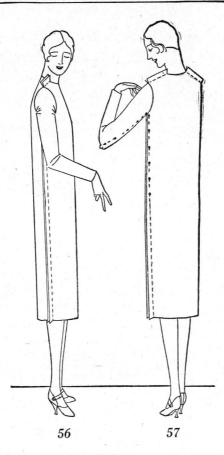

56   57

Altering Sleeves for an Arm Larger Than the Average

If the arm is only a little larger than the average, the sleeves can be adjusted very easily. Butterick Patterns provide "Outlet" or "Let-Out" seams. These seams are wider than the usual $\frac{3}{8}$ inch and can be let out $\frac{3}{8}$ of an inch on each side of the seam or a total of $\frac{3}{4}$ of an inch on each sleeve. This will make your sleeve too large for the armhole, but you can let out the underarm seam of the garment the same amount you let out the sleeve. The amount let out at the underarm seam of the garment can be tapered off gradually to nothing if you do not need the extra size at the hip.

Alterations for an arm decidedly larger than the average should be made in the pattern before the garment is cut. Directions for making these alterations are given on page 34.

Chapter V

MAKING YOUR GARMENT

THE *Pattern*—A Butterick Pattern is an exact copy of a garment which has been made up in fabric and tested on the human figure.

The Deltor—Wrapped up in every Butterick Pattern is a printed sheet of paper called the Deltor. This is not a stock sheet with general directions for cutting and constructing a garment, but a special sheet made for the special pattern you are using.

It is printed on both sides with pictures and words, and every picture and every word is put there to make it easy for you to construct this particular garment with the same good lines and expert finish that marked the model from which the pattern was cut.

Moreover, this printed matter is so arranged that you do not need to stop and read the entire sheet before beginning to cut out your material. Each detail, from the laying out of the pattern pieces to the putting in of the final stitch, is illustrated and described in the same order which was followed in the making of the model garment. If you will read and follow the directions and illustrations *in this order*, working step by step as the Deltor suggests, you will be assured of a perfectly made garment with a minimum of time and effort on your part.

Perforations and Notches

In order to make it possible for you to reproduce the design, it is necessary to use markings, such as notches and perforations, on the pattern, to indicate certain points in the cutting and making.

The position of each notch and perforation has been carefully studied and they have been placed at important points to guide you. The best result in the finished garment depends on careful marking of these locations on your materials and accurate use of these marks in basting the garment. It takes a little time to mark them, but you save the time over and over in the ease and accuracy with which you can put the garment together.

Large double perforations are used in cutting (Illustration 58). They show you how to lay the pattern on the right grain of your material. These large double perforations form a line, which is sometimes placed lengthwise, sometimes crosswise and sometimes on the bias of the material.

When they are laid on lengthwise, they are parallel to the selvedges.

When they are laid on crosswise, they run across the material from selvedge to selvedge.

When they are laid on the bias, it must be a true bias.

These large double perforations must be laid on the correct line of the material so that the garment will set well, and have the best effect when finished. If they are not placed exactly as directed or explained, and as shown in the layout on the Deltor of the pattern you are using, the garment will twist and look badly.

The large triple perforations also are used for cutting, but they are always laid on a fold of the material—a lengthwise, a crosswise, or a bias fold.

Illustration 58 shows a pattern laid on material with large double perforations on the lengthwise grain and large triple perforations on a lengthwise fold.

Before you pin your pattern on the material it is advisable to take a ruler or tape and measure to be sure that the lengthwise grain line is the same distance from the selvedge at each group of perforations.

Small double perforations are always used to mark the natural waistline in dresses, blouses, coats, etc. (Illustration 59.) In some cases they are also used to indicate the elbow or outlines of the neck, and are sometimes used in other special cases.

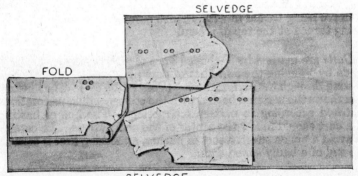

SELVEDGE

FOLD

SELVEDGE

58—Large double perforations on the lengthwise grain and large triple perforations on a lengthwise fold of material

Large single perforations and *small single perforations*, either alone or together, are used for different purposes, and their use is always shown in the Deltor.

"Outlet" or *"Let-Out"* seams are marked by large single perforations (Illustration 59). In basting them, the basting line should run exactly through the center of these perforations. "Outlet" or "Let-Out" seams are deeper than ordinary seams. They are made so on purpose, so that they can be let out if it is necessary to make any slight alteration to suit the individual figure. They are generally used at underarm and shoulder seams, and usually on the seams of sleeves. In so many cases women's shoulders are not exactly even, or there are other slight variations from the average at one point or another of the figure. These "Outlet" or "Let-Out" seams give you a chance to alter the garment in an easy, simple way. Consult the Deltor to find out where these seams are in the pattern you are using.

When basting up the garment for the first time, always baste through the center of the perforations that mark the "Outlet" or "Let-Out" seams and try the garment on. Then, if it is too tight at any part, rip the seams as required and rebaste to fit. Illustrations 59 and 60 show underarm, shoulder, and sleeve seams being basted through the outlet perforations.

Ordinary Seams are not marked by perforations, but are to be basted exactly ⅜ inch from the seam edge. This allowance of ⅜ inch is made on all edges except those that are to be cut on a fold of the goods, and, of course, except those that have the outlet or let-out allowance. In basting the garment *the seam lines must be followed exactly.* If you make any seam deeper or narrower, you will alter the size of the garment. Illustrations 61 and 62 show a sleeve being basted in with ⅜-inch seam and ⅜-inch allowance being turned at the top of a hem.

Darts are marked by V-shaped lines of perforations. A dart is made by bringing the two lines of dart perforations together and basting through the perforations. (Illustration 59.) The illustration shows the material basted with the corresponding perforations matched according to pattern instructions. The line of basting in a dart should follow the center of the perforations. Be careful to avoid a pouch effect, a sort of pucker, something that is seen at the end of a badly sewed dart.

Notches are used at seam edges to show which edges should be joined. Edges marked with notches are put together with the corresponding notches matching. (Illustrations 59, 60 and 62.)

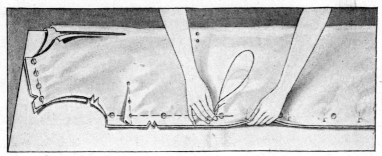

59—The first basting on "Outlet" or "Let-Out" seams should always follow the line of large single perforations

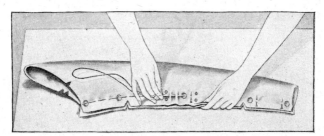

60—In basting sleeves be sure to baste directly through the "Outlet" or "Let-Out" perforations

61—An allowance of three-eighths of an inch is made for turning in the edge of a hem or facing

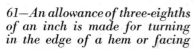

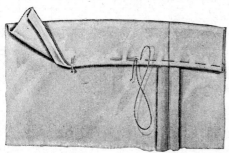

62—A sleeve is basted in with a three-eighths inch seam

Handling Materials

What You Should Know About Weaves and Design

Materials That Are the Same on Both Sides

Some materials, such as chambray, plain flannel and plain taffeta, are woven so that they have no distinct right and wrong and no distinct up and down.   Either side may be used as the right side, but it is always safer to cut your garment with the same side out on all pieces, because sometimes in sheen or color a slight difference will be apparent.

Materials With a Right and a Wrong Side

Many fabrics have some quality of weave or design that makes it important for you to be sure that you know the right from the wrong side of the goods, the up from the down of the weave or design.   With most fabrics of this kind the difference is unmistakable, but in some it is difficult to be sure.   The following information, based on the practises universally followed by textile manufacturers, will help you to determine these matters when there is any doubt.

Silks and woolens, when folded, are folded right side in.   When they are not folded, the inside of the bolt is the right side.

Cottons and linens, when folded, are folded right side out.   When they are not folded, the outside of the bolt is the right side.

The selvedge is smoother on the right side than on the wrong side.

In twilled materials, such as serge and diagonals, the twills run downward from left to right on the right side of the material.

Double-faced materials, such as crêpe satins and double-faced woolens, may be used with both sides out—that is, the garment may be made of the plain or shiny side and trimmed with the figured or dull side—or the other way around.

Determining the Up and Down of the Material

Nap or pile materials—Velvet, velveteen, panne velvet, corduroy, plush, and some wool fabrics, such as broadcloth, wool velvet and similar materials, have a distinct nap or pile—that is, threads cut off so that they produce a more or less furry or hairy effect. Such materials take the light one way with the nap or pile running down, and another way with the nap or pile running up. If all parts are not cut with these threads running the same way, the garment will look as though it were made from two shades of the same material.

With panne velvets, in which the pile is purposely flattened, it should run down; and white velvet is generally made up with the pile running in that direction. In broadcloth, too, the nap should run down; otherwise it will roughen up and become woolly.

Some velvets have straight pile with no up or down. They can be cut either way, but all the pieces should be cut the same way.

The other nap or pile materials should generally be used with the pile running up, so that it will fall out and show the full richness of the fabric. However, in some cases individuals prefer to have it run down, as this gives a smoother, more satiny surface.

How to Tell the Direction of the Nap or Pile

You can tell the direction of the nap or pile by running the palm of your hand lengthwise over the material. When the material feels rough, your hand is going against the pile; when the material feels smooth, you are rubbing with the pile.

Nap or Pile Materials in Kimono-Sleeved Garments

When kimono-sleeved garments are cut without a shoulder seam, it is impossible to have the pile run the same way at the front and back. In such a case, get the best effect possible at the front, as the back is less noticeable. In most of the pile fabrics let the nap run up in front; in broadcloth and panne velvet let it run down the front.

Following the Grain of the Material

The question of the grain or thread of the material is very important. All fabrics, except a very few that are made in tubular form, are finished on each side with a border called a selvedge. Woven materials are made with lengthwise and crosswise threads. The lengthwise (warp) threads run parallel to the selvedge. The crosswise (woof or weft) threads run across the warp and it is the turning back of the thread at the end of a line that makes the selvedge. (Illustration 63, page 61.)

In knitted materials there is no warp or woof. The fabric is built up a line at a time by pulling the thread through the stitches of the preceding line. In this way much the same effect is produced in the matter of grain as in woven materials; the lengthwise lines of chain-stitches representing the warp, and the crosswise ribs representing the woof.

To Get a Straight Grain

The only way to be sure of getting a perfectly straight grain is to follow a thread. In a loosely woven material or one with coarse threads this can be done by sight. When the fabric is too fine to make this possible, the lengthwise grain can be determined by measuring a definite number of inches from the selvedge at intervals and marking the line with pins or bastings.

To get a straight grain crosswise of the material the best way is to pull a thread in any fabric in which this is possible. To pull a thread, snip the selvedge and pick up a thread at the edge of the material. Pull the thread gently with the right hand, easing the material along on the thread with the left hand, thus allowing it to pull out without breaking. When the thread is pulled completely out, the open space will be an exact crosswise grain.

In fabrics where it is impossible to pull a thread, as in certain pile fabrics or materials with a woolly surface, the grain can be pretty accurately determined by feeling. Double the fabric over on a straight line, right sides together, lengthwise or crosswise, for about a quarter of a yard, and stretch the fold gently between the fingers. If it pulls unevenly, try shifting the fold until you get the effect of a straight line running from one hand to the other.

It is not possible to pull a thread in a knitted fabric because this would ravel and destroy the material; but the lengthwise or crosswise lines are usually easily followed with the eye. Where the fabric is too fine to show the grain easily, or is covered by a furry surface, as in the brushed-wool effects, the grain can usually be determined by feeling, as described in the preceding paragraph.

Some materials can be torn. Where this is possible it is sometimes better than cutting, as in the making of straight ruffles, sheets, wash skirts, or anything else that is to be washed, because this assures a perfectly straight edge after laundering. In the making of outer garments, however, it is usually better to depend upon your shears, making sure always that the pattern is laid accurately on the grain of the goods as indicated by the perforations in the pattern.

In printed materials it is sometimes necessary to follow the design instead of the grain of the goods in laying on a pattern, when, as sometimes happens, the design is not applied to accord with the grain. This must be done very carefully, however, because if the garment is to have hard wear, and especially if it is to be laundered, it will stretch out of shape and look badly.

A lengthwise fold is parallel to the selvedge. (Illustration 63.)

A *crosswise fold* is a fold made straight across the material from selvedge to selvedge.   (Illustration 63.)

A *true bias* runs diagonally across the material.   (Illustration 64.) It is obtained by spreading the material on the table and making a mark seven or eight inches from one corner on both the selvedge and the cut end, which must be cut on the crosswise grain.   Lay a yardstick across the corner, touching both these marks, and draw a line.   In cutting bias strips, make as many marks as there are strips needed, marking them the required width.   Then cut carefully, following the line and using sharp scissors.   Be careful to have the cut strips all on the same bias.

When bands, folds, ruffles, facings, etc., are made on the bias, they must be cut on a true bias to give satisfactory results.   To maintain a perfect bias, the strips should be of equal width throughout their entire length.

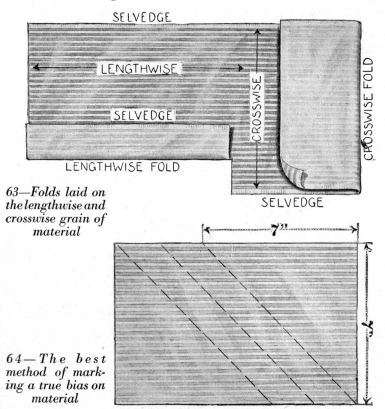

63—*Folds laid on the lengthwise and crosswise grain of material*

64—*The best method of marking a true bias on material*

To join bias strips—Lay the two ends together as shown in Illustration 65 and baste in a seam.   It will then be seen that when the joined strips are lapped back the grain of both pieces runs in the same direction.   (Illustration 66.)

When bias bands are called for in a Butterick Pattern, provision for cutting them is always made in the Deltor layouts.   Sometimes in remodeling a garment where it is necessary to get them out of small pieces there is a short cut that will save time and avoid the necessity of much piecing together.   Trim your piece even on all four sides, find the true bias, mark as many strips as can be cut from the piece, and cut off the triangular piece at one corner. Then pin two opposite edges together, leaving the beginning of the binding free and matching the other marks carefully as shown in Illustration 67.   Stitch the seam and begin to cut at the free end, following the line around and around the tube.   (Illustration 68)

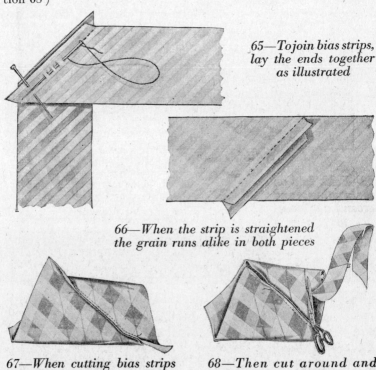

*65—To join bias strips,
lay the ends together
as illustrated*

*66—When the strip is straightened
the grain runs alike in both pieces*

*67—When cutting bias strips
from small pieces, join the
edges to make a tube*

*68—Then cut around and
around, following the line that
marks the true bias*

Laying Out Your Pattern

If the Deltor calls for an open lay—that is, with the material opened out to its full width—it is advisable to press out the center fold in fabrics that come folded. Whenever the Deltor layout calls for cutting on a fold, it is better, whenever possible, to use the fold already in the material. However, this is sometimes wasteful, as the fold indicated on the Deltor is not always directly in the middle of the material. In cases of this kind the material is opened in Deltor layouts so that it can be cut to better advantage.

When making a fold, be sure that the fold is true. Directions for finding the grain of the goods, either crosswise or lengthwise, as well as for getting a true bias, are given on the pages immediately preceding this. After you have found the line for your fold, pin it at short intervals to keep it even, and pin along the selvedges or around the outline of the pattern to make sure that the material does not slip during the cutting.

On the Deltor that accompanies every Butterick Pattern are "layouts" that have been worked out by skilled cutters. These have been prepared to save your time, and to make it easy for you to cut your garment from the smallest amount of material out of which it is possible to cut it without sacrificing the correctness of grain that is so essential to good lines in the finished garment.

The first thing to do, after you have spread your Deltor out with the layout side up, is to select the layout which meets your needs and for which you have bought the material.

For instance, suppose the pattern you are using is a size 36 dress pattern that shows on the envelope two pictures, one with short sleeves and one with long sleeves; and that you decided you wanted to make your dress with short sleeves, and bought the amount of 35-inch material, without up and down, which was given as necessary on the pattern envelope. The thing for you to do is to pick out on the Deltor the layout given for size 36, with short sleeves, to be cut from 35-inch material with no distinct up and down, and draw a pencil line around it, so that your eye can find it instantly as you look from your own pattern and material to the printed layout. This is the only layout to which you need pay any attention.

If you take a size 42 or 32, or any other size in which the pattern is made, and have bought the amount of 35 or 39 or 54 inch material with a distinct up and down listed as necessary for your size in the long-sleeved development of the pattern, look for the layout that is given for these requirements.

Then lay out your pattern pieces on your material exactly as they are shown in the printed layout and pin the pattern in place with small pins placed as close together as necessary to hold it firm.   Do not push the pins through the material recklessly, but use only the points and take up as few threads as possible so that the material will not be marked.   Always place a pin so that it will lie at right angles to any edge that is to be cut, or to any basting line that is to cross it.

The pinning of the pattern on to the material is very important. The edges that are to be placed on a fold must be on the fold, not inside or outside it; and the grain line must be carefully observed with every piece.

In cutting velvet, plush, corduroy or silk, be very careful in the use of pins.   Use very fine pins or needles.   Ordinary pins may make holes in thin silks and chiffons and scar velvets and other pile fabrics.

If the two sides of the garment are exactly alike, you will find that the pattern is for just half the garment, and that each piece is to be cut double or twice.   The front and back are usually cut double with the centers on a lengthwise or crosswise fold of the goods.

If one side of the garment is different from the other, a pattern piece is usually given for each part that is different.   Sometimes patterns give only one piece for a one-sided dress, the larger piece. To cut the other side, part of the pattern must be turned back according to instructions given on the pattern envelope and in the Deltor.

Cutting and Marking Perforations and Notches

In cutting, use sharp shears and follow the edge of the pattern exactly.   If you cut with small or dull scissors, you will get a jagged edge that is hard to follow accurately in basting.   When cutting materials that fray easily, allow an extra eighth of an inch on all ordinary three-eighths-inch seams, and do not forget this when basting.   No extra allowance is necessary on the "Outlet" or "Let-Out" seams.   As soon as you have cut the garment in such materials, overcast the armhole and neck edges to prevent raveling.

Before removing a pattern from the material, mark every notch or perforation that has to do with the construction of the garment. To do this, mark with tailors' tacks all perforations except the ones that mark the grain line.   (See pages 91 and 92 for method of making tailors' tacks.)   The notches can either be marked with two or three stitches in basting cotton or they can be marked with *small* nicks.   In many materials basting cotton makes a clearer mark and does away with the necessity of nicking the edge of the material.

Laying Out Stripes, Plaids and Figures

Stripes, lengthwise or crosswise, plaids and bordered or figured materials require more care in laying out than do plain materials.

In the beginning, decide which stripe, plaid or figure is best for the center of the front and back.

Fold the material lengthwise at the stripe, line or figure chosen for the center back.

It gives the best effect to have a heavy crosswise stripe come a short distance above the lower edge of the finished garment. Before cutting plaids or materials with crosswise lines, figure the length of the garment as carefully as possible so that the lower edge will not need to be changed.

Place the front and the back on the material with the lower corners of the underarm edges the same distance below a crosswise stripe. (Illustration 69, page 66.)

Place the sleeve on the material with the notches in the upper edge in the same relation to a crosswise stripe as the corresponding notches in the armhole of the front and back. To do this, place the upper edge of the sleeve pattern on the front and back sections of the pattern with the armhole notches matching, and mark on the pattern the crosswise stripe nearest to the notches. (Illustration 69.)

When the sleeve is laid on the material, lay the cuff pattern on it and mark the position of a stripe on the cuff pattern so the cuff can be cut to match the sleeve. (Illustration 70, page 67.)

To cut a pocket to match plaid on the front section of a garment, lay the pocket section of the pattern on the front and mark on the tissue the location of a stripe. (Illustration 70.)

If a stripe is used in the center back of a collar, it should be the same stripe that is used in the back of the garment.

After cutting one front, one sleeve, one cuff and one side of the collar, lay these pieces on the material with the right sides together, matching lengthwise and crosswise stripes, and cut the other half. Then lay the pattern on the cut sections of material again and mark all notches and perforations that are to be used in putting the garment together. (Illustration 71, page 68.)

Irregular Plaids, Wide Stripes and Large Figures

A dress made of irregular plaid, large plaid, wide-striped or large-figured material requires more material than one made of small plaid, narrow-striped or small-figured material, the amount depending on the size and arrangement of the figures or lines.

It must be borne in mind in laying out a pattern on an irregular plaid that all pieces of the pattern must be placed in the same direction on the material.

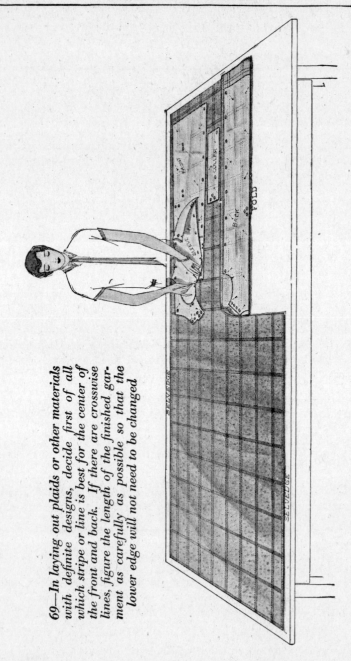

69—In laying out plaids or other materials with definite designs, decide first of all which stripe or line is best for the center of the front and back. If there are crosswise lines, figure the length of the finished garment as carefully as possible so that the lower edge will not need to be changed

70—*After the sleeve pattern has been marked so that the crosswise lines of the sleeve will meet those on the front and back, lay the cuff pattern on it and mark the position of a stripe or plaid so that the cuff can be cut to match the sleeve*

71—*After cutting one front, one sleeve, one cuff, etc., lay these pieces on the material with the right sides together, matching lengthwise and crosswise lines, and cut the other half. Then lay the pattern on the cut sections again and mark all notches and perforations that are to be used in putting the garment together*

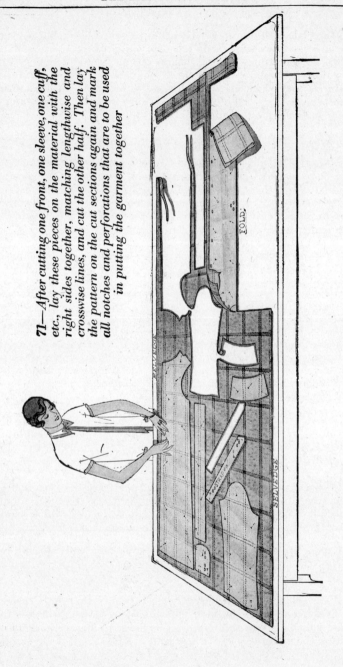

Materials with flowers or other figures so arranged that they give the effect of lines must be matched just as in the case of plaids and stripes. Sometimes figures run up on one line and down on the next line. In that case the pieces may be cut either way of the material; but when they all run the same way you must decide whether you want them to run up or down in your garment and use them in the same direction in every piece.

Putting Your Garment Together

After you have cut your garment according to the Deltor layout and have marked every perforation and notch that is needed for putting it together, look at the illustrations and directions given on the Deltor to guide you in the construction. Follow these, step by step, from the first basting to the finishing stitch, and your garment will go together easily and correctly.

A fine needle and silk thread should be used to baste silks and velvets, as cotton will often leave a mark on such fabrics.

Always test the machine-stitch on a scrap of the material that is to be stitched before beginning to sew the garment in order to be sure that the length of the stitch and the tension are correct. (See pages 78-81 for further suggestions about the use of the machine.)

When stitching velvets, plushes, and similar materials, loosen the tension on the machine and lighten the pressure of the presser-foot, following directions in your machine manual for making these adjustments.

In stitching sheer materials like chiffon, silk crêpe, crêpe de Chine, etc., that are likely to pucker while the stitching is being done, place a narrow strip of thin paper under the material and stitch through it. After the stitching is finished, it is easy to pull the paper apart along the line of stitching.

In stitching seams in which one portion is fulled on to another, place the full portion downward next to the feed, because if it is placed next to the presser-foot the foot may push the fulness out of place.

Except when they are finished in some way so that they form part of the decoration of a garment, seams should always be made as inconspicuous as possible.

When you are ready to take out your bastings, clip them every four or five inches, or even closer. Pulling long basting-threads from silks, velvets or fine thin materials is likely to make a bad mark or to tear the material.

Trimming Off "Outlet" or "Let-Out" Seams

Sometimes, as in a garment made of transparent material, or one that is to be finished with French seams, or in the underpart of a kimono sleeve where a wide seam would "draw," it is necessary to trim off the "Outlet" or "Let-Out" seams after the garment has been fitted.

In any case where they can be left their full size without impairing the appearance of the garment, we advise leaving them, as they provide a means of letting out the garment if the figure of the wearer should become larger.

Finishing Your Garment

The finish of a garment may perfect or destroy one that is correct in every other respect—line, cut and fit—and it is just as possible to spoil a garment by doing the finishing too carefully as by slighting it; for the finish of a garment is a thing that must be handled lightly and expertly, with just enough sewing to make seams and edges secure and trimmings lie smoothly or lightly, as the case may be.

A dress that is beautifully sewed may be hopelessly "home made" in effect because although the stitches are perfect there are too many of them or they are too firm for the material. Sometimes the sewing on a fragile evening dress is of the kind that is appropriate for household linen which must stand frequent and hard laundering.

Except where it is done as part of the trimming, sewing should never show on a dress. There should be just enough to keep the garment together and finish it properly, and the amount and kind of sewing that should be done on a given garment depend not only on the type of garment but on the fashion trend of the season.

The Guide to Good Finishing

For these special problems the Deltor that accompanies each Butterick Pattern supplies the detailed information that is necessary. It shows in pictures the easiest and best way to finish the garment both inside and outside so that it will look exactly like the original model from which it was made, and the finish illustrated is always in the mode and of the kind that is being used, at the time, in the best French and American dressmaking houses; and by following its directions and illustrations you can be assured of the finish that will make the dress or coat or blouse or bit of lingerie exactly *right* and in the mode.

Chapter VI

EQUIPMENT FOR DOING THE BEST DRESSMAKING

The Ideal Sewing-Room and What It Should Contain—Chest of Drawers—
Closet—Cutting-Table—Mirror—Small Equipment—Dress-Form—
Sewing-Machine

DRESSMAKING, like any other form of work, will give the best results when it is done with the best equipment. "Best" does not necessarily mean the most expensive. A pine table of the right height and size for cutting and sewing is a better table for dressmaking than a mahogany sewing-table just big enough to hold your scissors and work-basket.

The Ideal Sewing-Room and What It Should Contain

Every woman who sews or who has sewing done at home should, if possible, have a light, well-equipped sewing-room. It need not be large, but it should have a good light by day and the artificial light should be properly placed and shaded. When dressmaking is going on, the floor may be covered with a clean sheet or linen drugget—sometimes called a crum-cloth. This covering keeps light-colored material from becoming soiled and also makes it possible to leave the sewing-room in perfect order at the end of the day, for all the scraps and threads can be picked up in the cloth.

A chest of drawers is useful, one drawer for buttons, thread, sewing-silk, hooks and eyes, etc., another for patterns and a third for left-over pieces of materials. Keep all pieces of material as long as the garment is in use, in case you wish to mend or alter it.

There should be a closet with coat and skirt hangers, or hooks on the wall of the sewing-room with a curtain to draw over and protect from dust anything that is left hanging overnight.

The room should have a table at least 40 inches wide by 54 inches long. If it has a drawer or several drawers, you can keep your shears, pins, etc., there. (Illustration 72.)

The table should have a smooth, hard even surface and should be of a comfortable height so you can sit at it with your feet under it as you would sit at a writing-table. Never sew with your work

*72—Your sewing-room should have a table on which
you can cut out a garment or rest your work when
you are sewing by hand*

on your lap.   It makes you sit in a fatiguing position, strains your
eyes and back and stretches and crumples your work.   Lay your
sewing on the table, letting the table support its weight.

If it is not possible to have a permanent cutting-table, a dining-
table, extension style, enlarged, will give ample surface for cutting, or a folding table may be made 40 inches wide by 54 inches
long with legs that fold under and hinges at the center so that it
can be folded in half and put away in a closet.

Do not cut out on a bed, because the surface is too soft to keep
the material straight and the bed too low for comfortable work.

A full-length mirror is a great convenience in dressmaking because you see the full effect of your clothes when trying on.

Shears and scissors—Dressmaking shears should be about nine inches long. Never use small scissors for cutting out a garment. The shears should be kept well sharpened so that they will cut a clean, even edge and not fret and chew the material.

The best shears for dressmaking are known as the "bent" shears. (Illustration 72.) They are bent in this way so that they will raise the material as little as possible and will prevent the under layer from slipping where two thicknesses of material are being cut. Do not buy a cheap, poor pair. Good steel will last for many years.

Do not use your shears for cutting threads, etc. You will need a medium-sized pair of scissors and also a pair of buttonhole scissors.

Tape measure—Learn to use your tape measure accurately, for one of the points of fine dressmaking is the difference between an eighth of an inch and a quarter, a quarter of an inch and three-eights.

Pins—Clean, unbent pins are important. Small pins are better than large, and fine steel pins or needles should be used on silk or any material that will mark. Never push a pin through to its head. Use the points only and take up as little of the material as possible.

Needles of various sizes and kinds—The needle must be in proportion to the thread and to the texture of the material on which it is to be used. It should be just large enough for the thread to slip through the eye easily and heavy enough not to bend when it is put through the material. Pins and needles that are in use should be kept in a cushion.

Basting cotton and cottons in different colors for marking tailor's tacks, notches and perforations.

Thimble—Be sure it fits correctly.

Tailor's chalk to mark lines or the length of a dress or skirt.

Yardstick to measure the length of a dress or skirt.

Emery for polishing needles.

Stiletto to use when making eyelets.

Bodkin for running ribbons and tapes in insertion and casings.

The sewing-machine and the dress-form have been left to the end, not because they are of little importance but because they are of so much importance that each one has a chapter devoted to it.

Chapter VII
THE DRESS-FORM

IT IS necessary in dressmaking at home to have a perfect duplicate of your own figure on which you can try your clothes as
you make them.

Buy a good dress-form one size smaller than your bust measure.
For instance, if you have a thirty-six-inch bust, buy a thirty-
four-inch dress-form. The stand should be on casters so that you
can move it around and turn it easily. Adjust the form to your
own height.

Buy a close-fitting lining pattern reaching down to about the
hips, buying it by your bust measure, and a plain narrow skirt
pattern by your hip measure. Cut the waist lining and skirt from
unbleached muslin, natural-colored linen, duck or similar material
of firm, strong quality so that it will not stretch. It should be
thoroughly shrunk before it is used. In cutting the waist lining,
cut only one sleeve.

Put the body lining and skirt together according to the Deltors
given with the patterns, making the body closing at the center
front and the skirt closing on the left hip. Try on directly over
your corset so that you will get as close a duplicate of your figure as
possible. (In using the finished dress-form, remember that it represents your figure without lingerie, and dress the form in the
lingerie that you usually wear.) Make any necessary alterations at
the "Outlet" or "Let-Out" seams, fitting the lining very carefully. Be sure to have the neck and armhole exactly right.

Turn under ⅜-inch seam allowance at the upper edge of the
skirt, pinning the skirt to the body according to instructions given
in the Deltor, keeping centers of body and skirt together. Make
any necessary alterations at the seams or darts, being careful that
the skirt fits you perfectly. Turn up the bottom of the skirt at
the length you usually wear.

Separate the body lining and skirt. Stitch the lining seams directly through the bastings. If you can't remove them afterward, it
doesn't matter in this case. Press the seams open. It is not necessary to bind or overcast them. Run a strong basting thread

73—*A dress-form on which you can try your clothes as you make them*

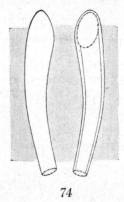

74—*Make one sleeve-form. You can use it for either sleeve*

73   74

around the armholes and neck to keep them from stretching, turning the neck edges under three-eighths of an inch. Stitch the fronts of the body lining about an eighth of an inch back of each fold edge. Mark the waistline by a line of colored thread through the waistline perforations. Stitch the skirt seams and press them open. Baste under the ⅜-inch seam at the top. Baste the bottom hem securely.

Make up the single sleeve you cut out, following the directions given with the pattern. Baste it into the lining and try it on to be sure that it is the right length and sets comfortably on the arm. Fit the sleeve as close to the arm as possible. Then rip the sleeve out. Stitch and press open the sleeve seams.

Place the body lining on the dress-form, leaving the front edges open temporarily. Pad between the lining and the form with tissue-paper, cotton rags or wadding until it fits perfectly. Be careful in padding, not to stretch or draw the lining or to let the padding get in bunches. Pad it until the front edges just meet (Illustration 75), and pin them together. Then sew them together with an overhand stitch.

If you have prominent or uneven hips or a round abdomen, place the wadding where it is needed. When you pad below the waist-line, pin the wadding to the form so that it will not slip. Be very particular about the hips. Pad them out so they are exactly like your figure.

When you have padded the form to its right proportions, turn up the lower edge of the body lining and cover the padding at the hips with a thin piece of lining material, tacking the covering to the dress-form to keep the padding in place. Then turn the edge of the body lining down over this covering. Place a piece of lining inside each armhole, stretching it flat across the opening. Turn in the armhole edges three-eighths of an inch and fell them to it. (Illustration 73.)

Place the skirt on the form, carefully pinning the upper edge and placket. Overhand the placket. Overhand the upper edge of the skirt to the body.

For a figure that varies quite decidedly from the average it is better to use a special dress-form. You can either make up the lining, send it to a firm that makes dress-forms and have a special form made from it, but a size smaller than your lining, or you can buy an adjustable dress-form and adjust it to represent your figure. In either case cover the form with your lining and pad it as directed.

A woman who sews for a number of people will have to use an adjustable form with a fitted lining for each person she sews for. Mark these linings distinctly with the name of the person for whom it was made. The form will have to be adjusted and padded each time a lining is used.

A dress or skirt can be put on the form and the form placed on the table when working on the lower part of a garment.

In fitting a coat, dress the form with the waist and skirt, or dress, over which the coat will be worn.

Sleeve-Form

Take the finished sleeve of the lining and pad it firmly and even-ly. Place a piece of lining material over the padding at the wrist, turn in the wrist edges three-eighths of an inch, and fell them to the piece of material. Slip a piece of lining material in the armhole of the sleeve. Turn in the edge of the under portion of the sleeve three-eighths of an inch and fell the edge to the lining material. Pad the upper part of the sleeve until it looks as nearly as possible like the arm. Turn in the upper edge of the piece of lining three-eighths of an inch and fell it to the upper part of the sleeve. (Illustration 74.) You can use the sleeve-form for either the right or left arm as it is not intended to be used for the actual fitting of the sleeves. This should be done on the arm. The sleeve-form will be useful in applying trimming or adjusting fulness in sleeves.

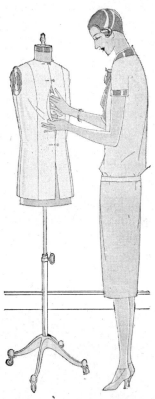

75—Be careful in padding the bust form not to stretch or draw the lining out of shape or let the padding get in bunches

Chapter VIII

THE SEWING-MACHINE

IT MAY be taken as a matter of course that any one who does dressmaking has a sewing-machine, but many people own machines for years and never learn how much a sewing-machine can accomplish, the many almost unbelievable things it will do and the real economy in its use.

Whatever make of machine you own, the company which made it is the best authority regarding its care and operation. Their book of instruction is your best aid in becoming thoroughly familiar with the machine itself, the places for oiling, the needed adjustments of needle, bobbin or tension screws, and especially with the various attachments that can be used for so many fascinating methods of finishing and trimming garments and accessories.

If you have bought a new machine, read the instruction book from beginning to end before using it. Then take a few pieces of material, thread up the machine and experiment. Try it out not only on plain stitching but with all the attachments, making yourself familiar with their possibilities.

If there are any points you do not understand, after reading your book of instructions, ask the personal instructor at the shop where you bought the machine to help you; or, if you are not near enough for this, write to the manufacturer and explain your difficulty.

If you have had a machine for some time, but are not getting the best results, begin as though it were new. Read the instruction book and then ask for any needed help from your local sewing-machine shop or from the manufacturer.

Sometimes just cleaning and oiling, tightening the belt, or re-adjusting the needles or tension will correct what seemed to be a serious difficulty; yet a small thing of this kind sometimes causes a machine to remain unused for long periods of time.

Keep your machine in a convenient place in the sewing-room so that it is always ready for emergency seams, for mending, and for the occasional readjustments of clothing that come so frequently, especially in homes where there are children.

*76—Keep your sewing-machine in a convenient place
in the sewing-room so that it is always ready for use*

Care and Adjustments

Cleaning and oiling—Sewing-machines require daily oiling and cleaning if they are being used continuously. If used only a few hours a day, cleaning and oiling once or twice a week is enough. Always remove all lint, dust, threads, etc., before oiling.

Length of stitch—The length of stitch should be regulated to suit the thread that is being used and the material that is being sewed. As a general rule, when stitching fine material, use a short stitch, lengthening your stitch to suit heavier fabrics.

Size of needle and thread—When the correct thread and proper size of needle are used in relation to the selected fabric, perfect stitching results.

If the needle is too fine for the thread, and for the material that is being sewed, it is likely to break when crossing a seam. If too large a needle is used on fine material, unnecessarily large. punctures will show in the finished work.

Regulating the tension—The tension is a very important factor in doing good stitching. Study this point in the manual that accompanies your machine and follow the instructions given for adjusting it.

Attachments

Practically all sewing-machines are supplied with attachments which permit the use of the machine in many operations formerly possible only in hand sewing.

Among the attachments that come with most machines are Binders, Hemmers, Rufflers and Tuckers. The possibilities of these various attachments should be studied in the instruction book and practised until you can use them easily. They will save many hours if expertly handled.

With some machines it is possible to buy additional attachments, such as a small electric light that can be attached to the arm so that it throws light directly on the sewing and on the needle. This can be used, of course, only where electric current is available.

Other interesting attachments that can be bought are darners, small hemstitchers for putting seams together or attaching hems or bindings, and a buttonhole worker that makes buttonholes of various sizes.

By studying the manual that accompanies your machine you will learn to make full use of all its possibilities. For instance, without the use of any attachment it is possible to do on almost any machine hemstitching that looks like hand-work. To accomplish this, draw threads as for hand-hemstitching; turn your hem and baste it so that the edge of the fold falls in the middle of the line from which the threads have been drawn instead of along its edge. Stitch close to the edge of the fold. If it is very fine material, use a short stitch, lengthening it to suit heavier fabrics. After the hem is stitched, take the work from the machine and gently pull the hem back so that the edge of the fold is brought close to the solid part of the material. This is especially good for fine fabrics, such as handkerchief linen.

Some Hints for Good Sewing

Keep the machine clean and well oiled.

Test the stitching on a spare piece of cloth before starting to sew.

In stitching seams, keep the material to the left of the presser foot, having the seam extend toward the right. This allows greater freedom in feeding material under the needle.

When stitching materials of different weights together, where the "give" in the fabric varies, use paper under your stitching. This is separated underneath as the stitching is done and is easily removed.

Have a pair of scissors always handy to clip threads, edges of materials, etc.

Never pull the material under the presser foot. If your machine is properly adjusted, all you need do is gently guide the fabric as it is stitched.

Use a thread that suits your fabric and fit the needle to the thread.

If you use bobbins, make sure that they are wound evenly and not too full. Avoid winding one color over another; the buried ends are likely to come out and cause trouble. Bobbins are inexpensive, and if you like to keep various colored threads wound and ready, it will pay you to have an adequate supply of bobbins.

Remember that in general, fine materials need a light tension, fine thread, fine needle and short stitch, and that all these factors should be adjusted to suit fabrics of greater weight.

Always bear in mind that a good machine deserves and rewards good care, and study your instruction book until you know how to handle your machine as the manufacturer designed it to be handled.

Chapter IX

PLAIN SEWING STITCHES

Knots—Bastings—Even Bastings—Uneven Bastings—Combination Bastings—
Diagonal Bastings—Running Stitch—Backstitch—The Half Backstitch—The
Combination Stitch—Overhanding—Overcasting—Catch-Stitch—Slant Hem-
ming Stitch—Straight Hemming Stitch—Blind Hemming—Slip-Stitch—Loose
French Tacks—Tailors' Tacks

TO MAKE a knot, hold the threaded needle in the right hand.
Take the end of the thread between the thumb and first
finger of the left hand, stretching the thread tightly. Wind
it around the top of the first finger, crossing it over the end held
between the finger and thumb. Roll the first finger down the ball
of the thumb about half an inch, carrying the thread with it, and
with the nail of the second finger push the knot thus formed to the
end of the thread. If a larger knot is required, wind the thread
around the finger twice.

Bastings are temporary stitches used to hold two or more pieces
of material together while putting in the permanent stitches. The
thread should be smooth and rather fine. Careful basting is essential to successful sewing and dressmaking. There are four
kinds of bastings. In each case the start is made with a knot on
the right side so that it may be easily removed.

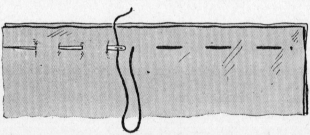

77—*Even bastings*

Even bastings—Pass the needle through the material, making the
stitches and spaces the same length. (Illustration 77.) To fasten
the thread at the end, take two stitches over the last one made.

82

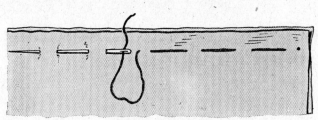

78—Uneven bastings

Uneven bastings are made by the method just described for even bastings, except that the stitches and spaces are of unequal length. The stitches taken upon the needle are about a third as long as the space covered by the thread on top. (Illustration 78.)

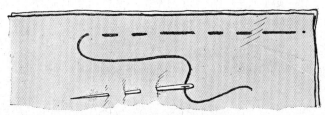

79—Combination bastings

Combination bastings are used on seams where extra firmness is desired for close fitting. They are made by taking alternately one long stitch and two short stitches. (Illustration 79.)

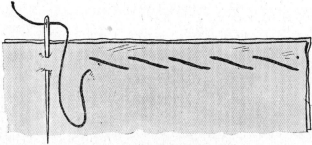

80—Diagonal bastings

Diagonal bastings are slanting stitches used to secure outside material to its lining, particularly where the lining is eased on to the material. The method is shown in Illustration 80.

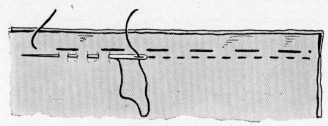

81—The running stitch

Running stitches are short stitches of equal length. They are used on seams that do not require the firmness of machine-stitching or backstitching. (Illustration 81.)

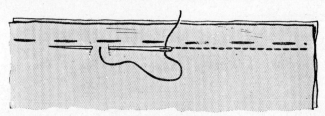

82—The backstitch

The backstitch is made by taking a short stitch back on the upper side and a longer one forward on the under side of the material. Insert the needle to meet the last stitch, passing it under the material and out again a space in advance of the last stitch taken. (Illustration 82.) Fasten by making two or three stitches over the one last made. The backstitch is used on seams requiring strength and firmness.

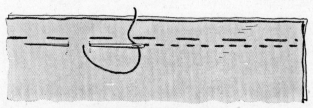

83—The half backstitch

The half backstitch is like the backstitch, except that the stitch is taken half-way back instead of all the way, leaving small spaces between stitches on the upper side. (Illustration 83.)

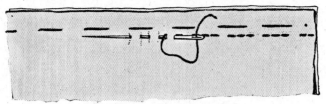

84—The combination stitch

The combination stitch consists of one backstitch and two or more running stitches. It is fastened like the backstitch. It is used on seams requiring a sewing less strong than the backstitch but stronger than running. (Illustration 84.)

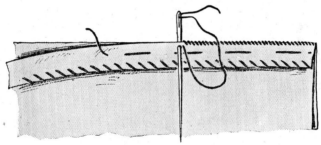

85—Overhanding

Overhanding, top sewing or oversewing, as it is sometimes called, is used to join folded edges or selvedges. (Illustration 85.) Baste the pieces with the folds or selvedges exactly even and sew with close stitches over and over the edges, taking up as few threads as possible, so that when finished the seam will be smooth and flat and not form an awkward ridge or cord on the wrong side.

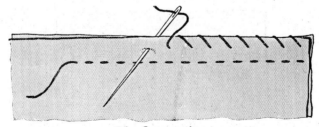

86—Overcasting

Overcasting is a slanting stitch used to keep raw edges from raveling. (Illustration 86.) In taking the stitch always point the needle toward the left shoulder. Hold the material loosely in the left hand.

Do not use a knot, but turn the end of the thread to the left and take the first two stitches over it. Make the stitches about one-eighth of an inch apart and one-eighth of an inch deep.

Keep the spaces between the stitches even and slant all the stitches in the same direction. Before overcasting, be sure that the edges are trimmed off evenly. In overcasting a bias seam, begin at the broad part of the piece and work toward the narrow part, to prevent its raveling while you are working on it.

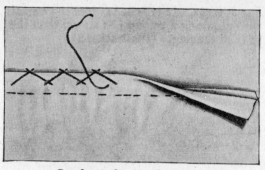

Catch-stitching a flat seam

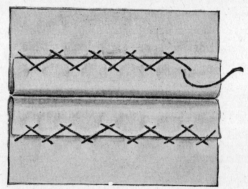

Catch-stitching an open seam

87—Two ways of using catch-stitching

Catch-stitch, sometimes called *cat-stitch*, is a cross-stitch used to hold down seam edges. It is the preferred finish for the seams of flannel garments, for it does away with the clumsiness of a French or felled seam, takes the place of overcasting and prevents raveling.

Place the edges together and run a seam, taking an occasional backstitch. Trim off one edge close to the line of sewing and press the other edge flat over it. (Illustration 87.)

Make a knot and insert the needle under the edge at the lower left corner, cross the edge and take a small stitch a few threads to the right. Cross back again and take a similar stitch through all the thicknesses of the material. Always point the needle to the left and make the cross-stitches encase the raw edges. The stitch is done from left to right.

If preferred, these seams may be pressed open and catch-stitched, working the stitches over the raw edge at each side of the seam, as shown in Illustration 87.

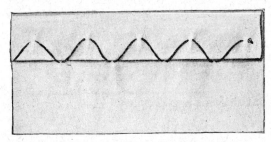

88—A quick method of catch-stitching

A quicker method of catch-stitching is shown in Illustration 88. This stitch has not the strength of the first method and is only used in millinery and in dressmaking where the work is concealed. This style of catch-stitching is done from right to left.

In hemming train the eye to keep the stitches even and true, take very small, almost invisible, stitches on the right side and stitches of an even length on the wrong side. Don't draw the thread tight, or leave it loose, and always use a fine needle and thread.

The slant hemming stitch is used to hold in place hems, facings, fells, etc. Each stitch slants on both the right and wrong side of the material. (Illustration 89.) Place the hem over the forefinger and under the middle finger of the left hand and hold it down with the thumb. Begin at the right hand and insert the needle through the fold, leaving a short end of the thread to be caught under the stitches.

Pointing the needle toward the left shoulder take a slanting stitch, taking up one or two threads of the material and the fold of

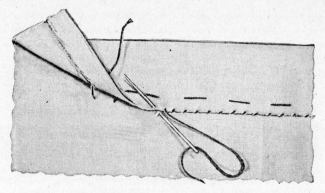

89—The slant hemming stitch

the hem.　At the end of the hem fasten the thread by taking two or three stitches on top of one another.

If a new thread is needed start as at the beginning, tucking both the ends of the new and old threads under the fold of the hem, and securing them with the hemming stitches.

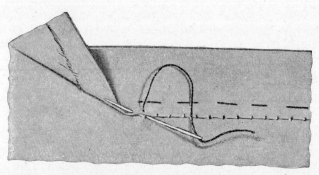

90—The straight hemming stitch

The straight hemming stitch is used where an edge is to be held close with stitches that should show as little as possible.　Start it the same way as the slant hemming stitch.

Insert the needle into the material as close to where you brought the thread through as possible, bringing the needle up in a slanting position under the hem and bringing it out through the fold of the hem close to the edge.　(Illustration 90.)　This is the stitch that is preferred by tailors for felling linings in coats, etc., for the stitches show less than in the slanting stitch.

Blind hemming is used when it is necessary to have the sewing invisible on the right side only. It is done more quickly than slip-stitching and is just as invisible on the right side of the garment. Take up only part of one thread in the material and insert the needle in the fold of the hem, using a rather long slanting stitch on

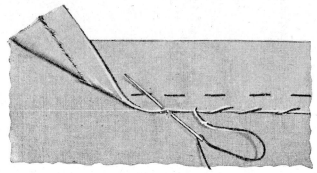

91—*Blind hemming*

the wrong side. (Illustration 91.) It is not a strong sewing but in many cases is used for hems or facings on silk and wool as it makes the impression of the hem least visible from the right side of the garment.

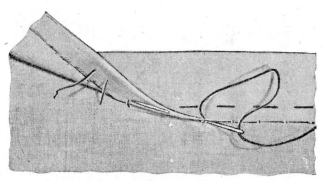

92—*Slip-stitching*

Slip-stitching is used when it is necessary to have sewing that is invisible on both sides, for holding hems, facings, trimmings, etc. It is not a strong sewing, but it is one of the most valuable stitches for finishing work in silk or wool. In this stitch it is necessary to take up only part of one thread in the material. This is what makes it invisible on the right side. The stitches should be taken as far apart as will hold the edge in place. Let the needle slip through the underside of the fold of the hem between the stitches and bring it out through the crease of the fold so that the thread does not show on the fold, thus making it invisible on the wrong side. (Illustration 92.) It is because the needle is slipped between the two layers of the fold that this is called the slip-stitch.

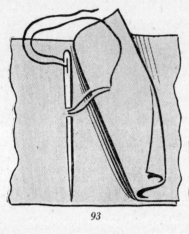

93

93—Three strands of thread between the parts that are to be held together, the first step in making a French tack

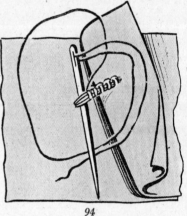

94

94—Working over the strands with several loose buttonhole-stitches to complete the process of making a French tack

Loose French tacks—These are made by taking a small stitch in the garment and one in the portion which is to be tacked to the garment, leaving a half-inch or more of thread between. Pass the needle back and forth again, putting it into the same place, and then work several loose buttonhole-stitches back over the three strands of the thread. (Illustrations 93 and 94.)

Tailors' tacks—After cutting out a garment by a pattern, before taking the pattern from the material, mark with tailors' tacks the perforations at "Outlet" or "Let-Out" seams and all other perforations that are to be used in putting the garment together (not the perforations used in cutting).

This will not take long and it will pay you many times over in time saved in basting the garment together. It is the only way you can be sure of getting your garment together just like the original model from which your pattern was made.

To avoid confusion when working, use a different color of thread for each kind of perforation. Use a double thread and do not make a knot. Take a stitch or two stitches (one over the other) through each perforation into both thicknesses of material.

If the perforations are less than 1½ inch apart, leave long loops of thread between the stitches. (Illustration 95.)

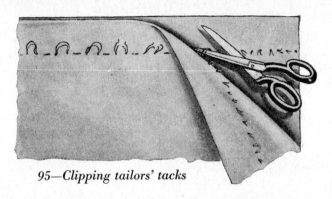

95—*Clipping tailors' tacks*

If the perforations are 1½ inch or more apart, the thread between need not be left in a loop, its length supplying the necessary thread for pulling through between the two pieces of material.

After all the perforations have been marked, clip the long threads and separate the pieces of material, cutting the threads that hold them together as you go along. (Illustration 95.)

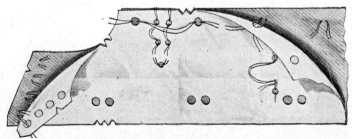

96—*Tailors' tacks on a garment where only one thickness of material needs to be marked*

If both sides of a garment are not alike and the perforations are to be marked in only one thickness of material, clip the threads between the perforations and take off the pattern. (Illustration 96.)

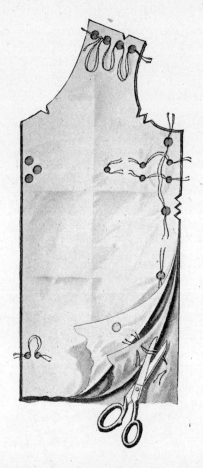

97—*Tailors' tacks on a garment where two thicknesses of material must be marked alike*

When a clean, exact line for sewing is to be marked through two pieces of material, or through both sides of a garment, baste through both thicknesses of the material alternating one long and one short stitch. Leave the long stitches loose enough to form a loop under which a finger can be passed. (Illustration 97.) Then cut every long stitch and separate the two pieces, cutting the threads that still hold them together as you go along. There will then be enough stitches in each piece to indicate the sewing line plainly and both pieces will be marked exactly alike. For any curved outline the tack stitches should be quite short.

Chapter X

SEAMS

French Seam—Turned-in French Seam—Fell French Seam—Flat Seam—
Lapped Fell Seam—Roll Seam—Dart Seam—Plain Seam Pinked—Plain
Seam Stitched—Plain Seam Bound—Joined Seams—Ordinary Tailored Seam—
Broad Seam—Cord or Tucked Seam—Welt Seam—Double-Stitched Welt
Seam—Open Welt Seam—Slot Seam—Double-Stitched Slot Seam—Strap Seam
—Lapped or Imitation Strap Seam—Raw Edge Lapped Seam

A SEAM is a joining of any two edges. The simplest form of
seam, made by laying the edges together and sewing with
one line of stitches on the wrong side, is used for temporary holding together, as in basting, or for a permanent seam.

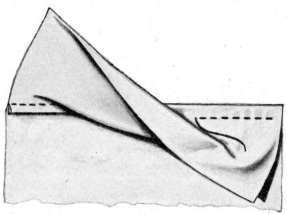

98—French seam

A French seam is a double seam used to encase raw seam edges.
Baste the two edges evenly together on the right side of the garment and sew close to the edge. (Illustration 98.) Trim off the
ravelings and turn the wrong side of the garment toward you,
creasing at the seam. Make the second sewing a sufficient depth
to cover the raw edges. (Illustration 98.) This seam is used for

thin materials and for dainty garments where it is not desirable to
show stitching on the right side.   It should be used on edges that
are easily turned and that are not bulky.

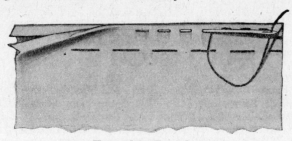

99—Turned-in French seam

A turned-in French seam is used when the lines of a garment are
such that this seam is more practical than the regular French seam.
It is used on edges that are very much curved, and on edges that
have been basted at the finished sewing line and can be finished
more easily this way.   Make a plain seam on the wrong side of
the garment.   Turn in both edges of the seam toward each other,
turning each side the same amount.   (Illustration 99.)   Baste
the edges together and stitch them or finish them by top-stitch-
ing.   (Page 99.)

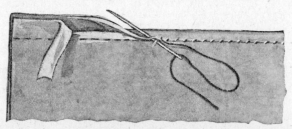

100—Fell French seam

A fell French seam is made with the usual plain seam on the
wrong side of the garment.   Trim off the edge that is toward you
to ⅛ inch in width.   Turn the other edge toward you ⅛ inch and
bring it to the seam line.   (Illustration 100.)   Finish it with a
hemming stitch or with small running stitches or by machine.

A flat fell or stitched seam has one edge hemmed or stitched down
covering the other raw edge.   It is used principally for wash gar-

ments, such as muslin underwear made in medium-weight materials, for flannels, tailored waists and working aprons.

Baste the seam edges together on the wrong side of the garment and sew the seam with combination stitch or stitch by machine. If the edges are bias, sew from the broad part of the piece to the narrow part to prevent the material from raveling and stretching.

Remove the bastings and trim the edge toward you to ⅛ inch. (Illustration 101.) Turn the other edge flat over it, pressing hard with the thumb-nail. Make a narrow turn, baste and hem or stitch by machine.

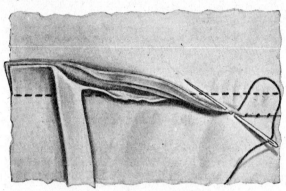

101—Flat fell or stitched seam

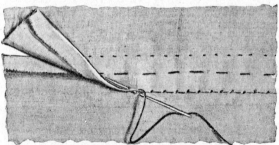

102—Lapped fell or stitched seam

A lapped fell or stitched seam is used on flannels, tailored waists or where there is no right or wrong side. Lap one edge of the seam over the other with the edges facing in opposite directions and with the seam lines exactly over each other. Baste through the seam lines. Trim off the ravelings from the edges and turn the edges under so that they meet. (Illustration 102.) The edge on each side may be sewed with a hemming stitch or by machine.

A rolled seam is used in sheer materials where an unusually narrow joining is required, and the material is likely to ravel or fray. Baste the seam edges together and trim off all the ravelings. Begin at the right end and roll the edges tightly between the thumb and forefinger of the left hand keeping the edges rolled for about 1½ inch ahead of the sewing. Whip the roll very close together, making the stitches come under the roll and not through it. Draw the thread tight. (Illustration 103.)

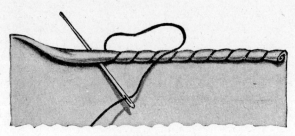

103—Rolled seam

Dart with fulness on one side—This dart is often used across the hip of a one-piece dress to put more width in the lower part than is in the upper. (Illustration 110.) It is sometimes used at the bust for the same purpose.

To make this dart so the edges will not pull apart or form a pout at the end when finished, it is necessary to sew a stay along the outline of the dart before it is slashed.

Cut for the stay a straight piece of the material ¾ inch wider than the wide end of the dart and ½ inch longer than the dart.

Place the stay over the dart marks on the garment (right sides together) with the edges of the stay an equal distance beyond the dart marks. (Illustration 104.) Baste the stay to position.

Turn to the wrong side of the garment and sew or stitch through the marks for the dart. (Illustration 105.)

Slash midway between the stitchings to an eighth of an inch from the end of the stitching. (Illustration 106.)

Turn the stay to the inside of the garment, turning it along the stitching on the longer side and basting the seam in the edge on the shorter side. (Illustration 107.)

Gather the longer side of the slash ⅜ inch from the edge where there is no stay and along the seam joining the stay to the garment. (Illustration 108.)

Lap the plain edge of the slash over the gathered edge with the edge meeting the gathers and baste. (Illustration 109.)

This dart is sometimes stitched on the outside or machine-hemstitched, depending on the material and the effect desired.

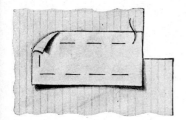

104—Baste the stay in place

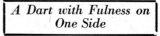

A Dart with Fulness on One Side

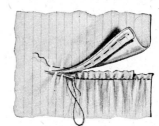

108—Gather the long side

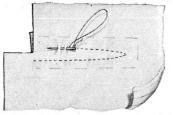

105—Sew around the dart

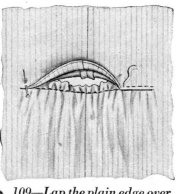

109—Lap the plain edge over

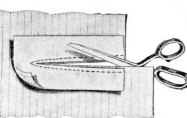

106—Cut between the lines

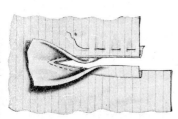

107—Turn in the stay

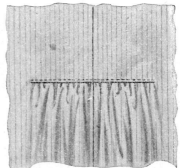

110—The finished dart

Tailored Seams

In tailored garments keep the cloth smooth at the seams, make the stitching as even as possible, and press carefully.

One should be very careful in deciding on the style of seam used on a tailored garment. To have a good tailored look the machine-stitchings on any seam must not be too fine. The thread and needle should be of medium thickness and the stitch should correspond in size.

Plain seams pinked—In plain seams of a closely woven material that does not fray or ravel, the edges of the seams may be simply notched or pinked and pressed open. (Illustration 111.)

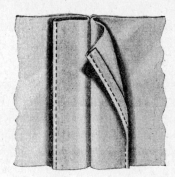

111—Plain seams pinked   *112—Plain seams stitched*

Plain seams stitched—In plain seams of silk or light-weight wools, the edges may be turned under and stitched close to the turning (not through the garment). (Illustration 112.) Press open.

Plain seams bound—Plain seams of jackets, cloaks and other garments made of heavy material that will fray should be bound with satin, silk, sateen or seam binding.

The materials should be cut in bias strips an inch wide. Stitch the bias on the right side of the seam edge ¼ inch from the edge. Hold the bias easy so there is no danger of drawing the edge. Turn the bias over the seam edge and stitch just inside the first stitching. If a seam to be bound is curved, it should be pressed before binding. After pressing, the seam will have spread at the edges and the binding can be safely applied without any chance of its pulling later.

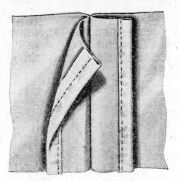

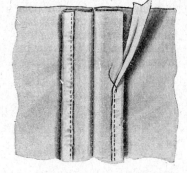

113—Bound with bias strips   *114—Bound with seam binding*

Seam binding should be wide enough to cover the edge nicely. Fold the binding with one edge a trifle shorter than the other, press it with a warm iron. Slip the binding over the edge of the seam with the shorter edge toward you, hold the binding a little easy so that there is no danger of drawing the edge. Sew the binding on with a running stitch or stitch it by machine, catching the edge of the binding on both sides of the seam edge. (Illustration 114.)

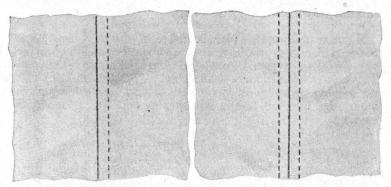

115—Edges turned one way   *116—Opened and stitched*

Joined seams of garments in which the lining and outer sections are stitched together are finished by turning in the raw edges of cloth and lining toward each other and closing the edge with overhand or running stitches. Where the seam is curved, the edges must be notched to prevent the garment from pulling.

An ordinary tailored seam which makes a good, neat finish is the plain seam pressed with both edges turned to one side, and a row of machine-stitching run in neatly along one side of the seam from the right side of the garment as shown in Illustration 115. Or, if preferred, a row of stitching may be applied to each side of the seam. (Illustration 116.)   In the latter case, however, the seam should be pressed open before running in the stitching.

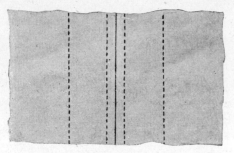
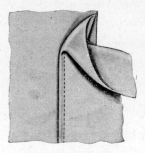

117—Broad seam   118—Cord seam

A broad seam is a plain, wide seam with four rows of ornamental stitching. (Illustration 117.) This seam is mostly used on tailored garments of heavy materials.

A cord or tuck seam is a plain basted seam with both edges turned to one side, and a row of stitching run about one-eighth of an inch or more from the seam, through the three thicknesses of the goods. This creates a raised or cord-like effect. (Illustration 118.) The undesirable thickness on the underside may be cut away at the inner edge as close to the stitching as possible. Remove the bastings.

119—Ordinary welt seam   120—Double stitched welt

A welt seam is made by first stitching a plain seam with one edge of the material left very narrow. Then turn back the fold and baste down close along the narrower seam edge. Stitch parallel to the line of bastings, keeping the seam flat. Illustration 119 shows this seam with the machine-stitches ripped out at the top to expose the narrow seam edge underneath.

A double- stitched welt seam has an additional row of stitching set in one-fourth inch more or less from the edge. (Illustration 120.)

121—Open welt   122—Reverse side of slot seam

An open welt seam—The edge is first turned under according to the instructions given in the Deltor and basted. The under edge is then placed with raw edges even and basted. With one row of machine-stitching the tuck-like fold and the seam are made secure. (Illustration 121.)

A slot seam is made by basting the seam as for a plain seam. The basting stitches should be short enough to keep the seam firm while it is being pressed open. Then baste an understrip of the material, a trifle narrower than the combined width of the seam edges, directly under the basted seam. (Illustration 122.) From the right side, stitch the desired width on each side of the center. Remove the bastings. The turned edges, now free, give the slot appearance, whence the name.

A double-stitched slot seam is produced by stitching another row each side of the center close to the turned edges. (Illustration 123.)

Strap seams are plain seams over which straps of the material are stitched for ornamental purposes. The strips for these straps may be cut lengthwise of plain material from pieces that are left after cutting out the garment, but experience has taught that when silk is used it is better to cut them on the bias, and when the material is cloth the better result will be obtained if the straps are cut crosswise or bias of the goods.

For a finished strap that is five-eighths of an inch wide, the strips are cut one and one-fourth inch wide. Join the two raw edges with loose overhand stitches as shown in Illustration 285, page 170, spread out the strap with the line of joining directly on the center and press.

When making strap seams it is desirable to graduate the thickness at the seam as much as possible. For this reason, cut the seams either wide enough so the edges on the underside will extend beyond the edges of the strap, or cut them narrower so the edges of the strap will extend beyond the seam edges.

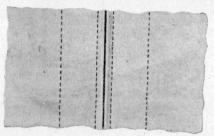

123—Double stitched slot seam

124—Strap seam

Baste the straps carefully over the seams, with a line of bastings run along each edge and stitch. (Illustration 124.) When it is necessary to piece the straps for long seams, avoid having the joining seam in a prominent place on the garment.

125—Imitation strap seam

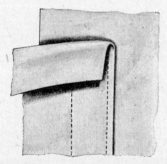

126—Raw-edge lapped seam

A lapped or imitation strap seam is the most practical finish for unlined garments. The edges at the seams are lapped and the raw edges turned in with a row of stitches finishing it alike on the right and wrong sides. (Illustration 125.)

A raw-edge lapped seam is used in making garments of heavy, closely woven material that will not fray or ravel. The seam edges must be cut very accurately and smoothly. Baste the edges evenly, lapping them the full allowance, and stitch as near the edge of the upper lap as possible. A second row of stitching five-eighths of an inch from the first gives it a neat and tailored finish. The seam on the underside should be trimmed off evenly. (Illustration 126.)

When trimming is applied over seams, the plain seam is used. It should be finished and pressed before the trimming is added.

Chapter XI

HEMS

Napery or Damask Hem—French Hem—Square Corners—Mitered Corners—
Circular Hem—Plain Hem—Rolled Hem

A HEM is a finish for the edges of garments, household linens, etc. It is made by turning the edge of the material over twice. (Illustration 127.) The first turning should be narrow and must of course be perfectly even. The depth of the second turning depends on where the hem is used and the effect you want to give. To make the second turning the same depth throughout its length use as a marker a card notched the desired depth of the hem. (Illustration 127.) If the hem is wide baste it at both the top and bottom.

A closer stitch is used in hemming household linens than in hemming garments.

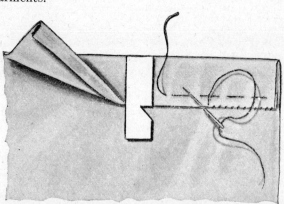

127—A card notched at the desired depth makes
an accurate hem gage

A *napery or damask hem* is used on napkins and table-cloths. Turn under the edge of the material twice for a narrow hem on a napkin. Fold a wider hem for a table-cloth. Fold the hem back on the right side, crease the material along the first fold, and overhand the fold and crease together. The needle is inserted straight, as shown in Illustration 128. Open and flatten the stitches with the thumb-nail. If a square is used, turn the opposite side in the same manner and hem before folding back the other two sides. No basting is needed for this hem. Take small stitches so that the work will look well when the hem is turned down.

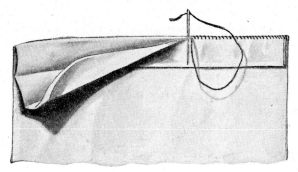

128—*A napery or damask hem*

Square corners are used in hemming squares or oblongs. Turn under the hem on one edge and then turn under the hem on the edge at right angles with the first. Crease the line where the fold of the second hem crosses the first hem. Open both hems and cut away the first hem to within a seam's width of the crease and the fold of the hem. (Illustration 129.) Turn under the hems again and hem the overlapping edges of the second hem to the underside of the first hem (Illustration 130) but not through to the right side.

129—*A hem creased and cut out to make a square corner*

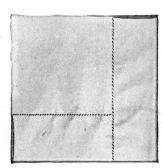

130—*The square corner as it looks on the wrong side*

Mitered corners also are used for squares or oblongs. They are made by joining two bias edges to form an angle. Turn the edges as for square hems and crease. Open the material, fold the corner toward the center and crease where the lines cross. Cut the corner off, allowing a narrow turning (Illustration 131). Fold the hems down all around, bring the mitered corners together and hem the side (Illustration 132). Hem the corners, but do not catch the stitches through the material underneath.

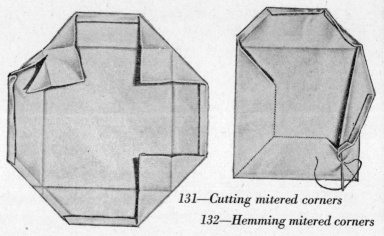

131—*Cutting mitered corners*

132—*Hemming mitered corners*

French hem—The seams must be stitched to within twice the depth of the finished hem, as shown in Illustration 133. Clip the seam at this point straight in to the line of the stitching, turn the seam edges toward the right side and stitch the remainder of the seam. Press open, turn the hem to the right side, baste and feather-stitch (Illustration 134), or finish in any desirable way.

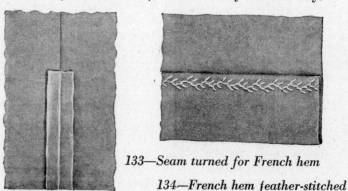

133—*Seam turned for French hem*

134—*French hem feather-stitched*

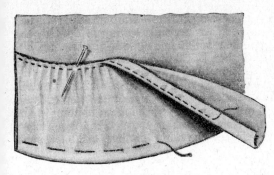

135—Top of a circular hem turned in and gathered

136 — Top of a circular hem finished with binding

A circular hem is often used on a garment that does not follow the grain of the material at the lower edge.

If the material is soft in texture, the top of the hem is simply turned under and a gathering-thread run in close to the turning. (Illustration 135.) Draw the gathering-thread till the top of the hem is the same size as the part to which it is to be sewed. Blind-stitch it or machine-stitch it to the garment.

If the material of the garment is of heavy weight the upper edge should be gathered without turning it under and the raw edge should be covered with a strip of seam-binding. (Illustration 136.) The lower edge of this seam-binding should be sewed to the hem but not to the garment.

Before sewing the top of the hem in place, slip a piece of muslin, cut the shape of the bottom of the garment, under the hem and press the hem flat, shrinking out as much of the fulness as possible. The piece of muslin will prevent the fulness in the hem from making marks on the garment during the pressing. The piece of muslin need not be the full width or size of the garment or hem. It can be a comparatively short piece and can be moved as the pressing is done.

After the hem has been pressed in this manner, hem the upper edge of the seam binding to the garment with invisible stitches.

A hem for a slightly gored or straight skirt—The hem edge is turned under in the usual way. If an invisible sewing is desired, the turned-under edge of the hem is stitched close to the turning, but not to the garment, and then blindstitched neatly and carefully to the garment. (Illustration 137.)

A straight hem can be finished with ribbon seam binding on silk or wool materials, and with bias-fold tape on heavy cottons or linen. Turn up the hem and stitch the edge of the seam binding to the upper edge of the hem without stitching through to the garment. Blindstitch the other edge of the seam binding to the garment. (Illustration 138.)

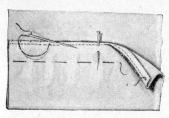
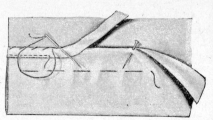

137—*Edge of straight hem turned in and stitched*   138—*Edge of straight hem bound with ribbon or bias fold tape*

A rolled hem makes a very pretty finish for bias or straight edges. It can be used only on an edge that makes a straight line. It can not be used on a curved edge.

An allowance of one and a half inches, more or less according to finished width desired, will have to be made on the edge for this hem. Turn the edge up on the right side and sew one-quarter of an inch more or less from the fold (Illustration 139). Then turn under the raw edge and hem it over the stitches on the wrong side. The hem must look round like a cord when finished—not flat.

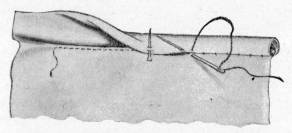

139—*A rolled hem for bias or straight edges*

Chapter XII

FACINGS

False Hem or Facing—Straight Facing—Bias Facing—Shaped Facing—Sewed-On Facing—Applied Facing—Extension Facing—Sewed-On Extension Facing—Applied Extension Facing—Corded Facing—Piped Facing—Facing a Slashed Opening

A FALSE hem or facing is often used for the finish of an edge. A garment can sometimes be cut from less material by using a facing, for a hem requires extra length or width while a facing can often be cut from pieces which would not otherwise be used. A hem is usually better than a facing for transparent materials as the joining seam shows through and does not look well unless the edge is trimmed in some manner that conceals the seam. Facings may be sewed to an edge and then turned, or the edge may be turned first and the facing applied.

A straight facing may be used if the edge to be faced is a perfectly straight line. The facing may be cut lengthwise or crosswise of the material.

A bias facing is used if the edge to be faced is slightly curved, for the bias facing can be stretched to fit the shape of the edge. To stretch the facing press it, stretching it at the outer edge and shrinking the inner edge as you do so. (Illustration 140.)

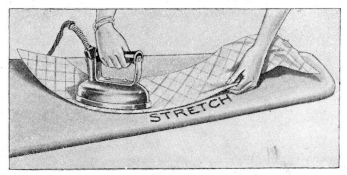

140—Stretching a bias facing to fit a curve

A shaped facing is cut the same shape and on the same grain of the material as the part to be faced. It may be used on all edges which are curved or irregular.

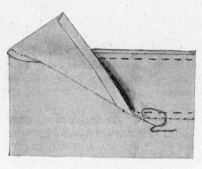

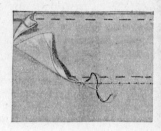

141—*Sewed-on facing*   142—*Applied facing*

The sewed-on facing—Piece the facing strips together and press the seams open. Baste and stitch the facing to the edge with the right sides together. Turn the facing over to the wrong side and baste it down flat along the edge, drawing the seam about ⅛ inch from the fold. (Illustration 141.) Baste again along the inner edge of the facing, turning in a narrow seam, or cover the edge with seam-binding.

The applied facing—Turn under one or both edges of the facing, baste and press. Turn under the edge of the garment and baste it. If the edge draws, clip it to make it lie flat. Baste the edge of the facing about ⅛ inch from the edge of the garment; then baste along the inner edge of the facing. (Illustration 142.)

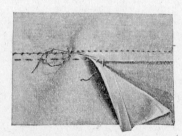

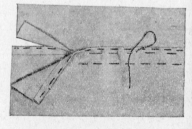

143—*Sewed-on extension*   144—*Applied extension*
        facing   *facing*

An extension facing may be used on any edge which is a straight line, or which is nearly a straight line, so that the facing can be eased enough to make it lie flat, but not so much that the easing will show after pressing.

The sewed-on extension facing—Cut a facing twice the width the facing should be when finished, plus a seam allowance on each edge. Baste and stitch the facing to the edge with right sides together. Turn under the loose edge of the facing and baste and hem it to the wrong side of the garment. (Illustration 143.)

The applied extension facing—Turn under all edges of the facing and baste them. Fold the facing through the center and baste it a short distance from the edge with the edges even. Slip the edge of the garment between the edges of the facing and baste. (Illustration 144.)

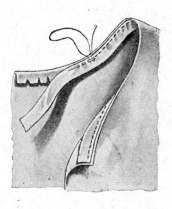

145—*Method of applying a corded facing*   146—*Ribbon seam binding used for facing*

To apply a piped facing—The method of applying a piped facing is exactly the same as with a corded facing. The cord is simply omitted.

To apply a corded facing—Turn under the edge you are going to face as allowed for on the pattern and baste it. Baste the facing flat to the inside of the edge with just the cording extending beyond the edge. A cord is put in a facing the same way it is put in a cord piping. (Page 166.)

Baste from the right side so that you can see what you are doing.

(Illustration 145.) Slip-stitch the cord in place with invisible stitches just under the edge of the garment. (Illustration 145.) The free edge of the facing should be turned under a seam's width or, if the material does not fray, it may be pinked and, if necessary, stretched to fit the edge of the garment. If an invisible sewing is desired the turned-under edge of the facing is stitched close to the turning, *not to the garment*. It simply lies flat against the garment. It does away with the second sewing of the facing to the garment, a thing that few amateurs can do invisibly.

Ribbon seam binding used for facing—Turn under the edge to be finished. If curved, clip it to make it lie flat. Sew the seam binding with a running stitch easing the straight edge to the curved edge to make it lie flat. Tack the inner edge invisibly. (Illustration 146.)

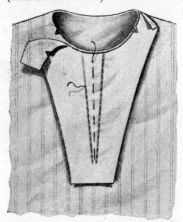   

147—Facing applied to outside   148—Slashed and turned to inside

Facing a slashed opening—Do not slash until the facing is on. Cut and baste the facing to the garment following instructions given in the Deltor. This opening being simply a slash where no seam allowance can be made, it is necessary to taper the sewing from ⅜ inch each side of the center at the neck to ⅛ inch at lower end of opening in order to have the lower end of opening as nearly a point as possible. To keep the stitching in a straight line, draw a line with tailors' chalk and a ruler and stitch on the chalk line. Cut through the center almost to the lower end of the stitching. Turn the facing to the wrong side with seam in edge and baste. Turn in the inner edge of the facing and stitch close to the turning but not to the garment. Tack the facing to the garment at intervals.

Chapter XIII

COLLARS, CUFFS AND BELTS

Unlined Collars—Lined Collars—Removable Collars—Unlined Cuff—Lined Cuff—Removable Cuff—Making and Finishing a Mannish Cuff—Sewing in Sleeves—Belts—Casings

COLLARS may be unlined or lined according to the material and the effect desired. The collar should be basted to the neck and tried on to make sure the size is exactly right. Then it should be ripped off and the outer edges finished or trimmed according to the style of the garment.

Collars for Garments Made of Material That Is Not Transparent

To sew an unlined collar to a garment of material which is not transparent, baste the collar to the neck with the underside of the collar against the right side of the garment.

Baste a narrow bias strip of material along the edge of the collar with the edges even. Stitch the seam and clip it at intervals so that it will not draw the neck (Illustration 149).

Turn under the edge of the facing and, if the collar extends all around the neck, hem the facing to the garment covering the seam. If the collar does not extend all around the neck edges, as in Illustration 149, finish that part of the neck which is beyond the collar according to the instructions given in the Deltor of the pattern you are using.

Seam binding may be used instead of a facing. It should be sewed on flat as in Illustration 150. Put it on so that the lower edge is not tight on the garment, easing the upper edge in wherever it is necessary to make it lie flat.

To make and sew a lined collar to a garment of material which is not transparent, where no part of the collar joining rolls to the outside and shows, baste and stitch sections with right sides together (Illustration 151). Turn right side out—baste and press with seam in edge (Illustration 152). Baste collar to neck and finish neck edge the same as for an unlined collar (Illustrations 149 and 150).

113

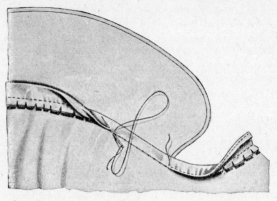

149—Stitch on a bias facing and hem it down to cover the joining of a collar to a garment that is not transparent

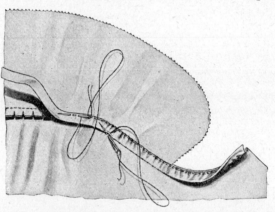

150—Or, if you prefer, stitch the collar on first and cover the joining with ribbon seam binding sewed on flat

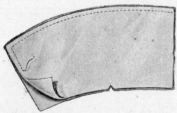

151—Stitch sections of a lined collar with right sides together

152—Turn it right side out and baste with seam in edge

To sew a lined collar to a garment of material which is not transparent where part of the collar joining rolls to the outside and shows, make collar as for a neck which does not roll open (Illustrations 151 and 152). Baste and stitch the upper section to the neck. Turn in under section and slip-stitch to cover the seam (Illustrations 153 and 154).

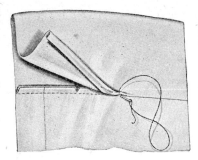

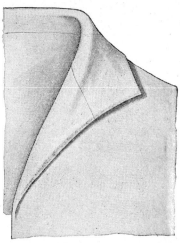

153—*Outer side view of a garment of material that is not transparent, showing the under section of a lined collar being slip-stitched over the seam that joins the upper collar section to the neck edge*

154—*Front view showing the collar rolled to the outside*

Collars for Garments Made of Transparent Material

When a single collar is to be joined to a garment of a material sufficiently transparent for the joining to show through to the outside, or if part of the collar joining rolls to the outside and shows, the daintiest effect is given by machine-hemstitching the seam. (Illustration 289, page 172.)

If the collar is double and part of the collar joining rolls to the outside, both edges of the collar should be basted to the garment with the seam toward the outside of the garment.

If the collar joining does not roll to the outside, the joining can be made with a narrow flat fell seam. (Page 94.)

A single or double collar should never be joined to the neck of transparent garment with a facing, for it makes a thick seam which will show on the outside.

It is advisable if possible to avoid a seam in the edge of either single or double collars in a transparent material.

Removable Collars

A removable collar for the open neck of a garment not made of sheer material is usually finished with a bias binding about ½ inch wide when finished. Turn in the edges of the binding ⅜ inch, fold through the center and press. Slip the neck edge of the collar between the edges of the binding and stitch.

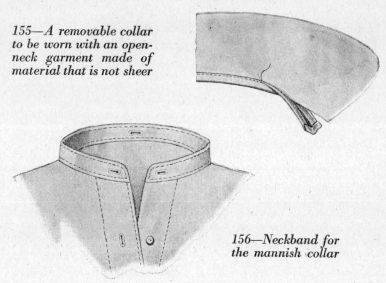

155—A removable collar to be worn with an open-neck garment made of material that is not sheer

156—Neckband for the mannish collar

The mannish neckband—The neck requires care. It should not be trimmed out too much and the neckband should fit the neck closely, though not too tightly, or it will be difficult to adjust the collar. An interlining should be used in the neckband. In most cases it should be of a material about the same weight as the garment material. The material of the garment can often be used for an interlining. In wash materials and flannel a soft cambric makes a good interlining.

The mannish collar—An interlining in a collar gives a more mannish effect. It may be used or not according to the degree of mannishness of the garment.

If a detached collar is desired, cut two sections and an interlining by the collar pattern. Stitch together on the outside edges. Turn, and baste the bottom of the collar and its band with the seam toward the wrong side, and then stitch. Hem the outer edge over to the line of stitching. Stitch around the outside of the collar and work buttonholes corresponding to those on the neckband.

Cuffs

An unlined cuff is sewed on a dress sleeve in the same way as an unlined collar. (Illustrations 149 and 150.)

A lined cuff which turns back is sewed on in the same way as a lined collar. (Illustration 153.)

A removable cuff is finished in the same way as a removable collar. (Illustration 155.)

The Mannish Cuff

For the slash in the sleeve sew the underlap piece to the back edge of the slash with the seam toward the right side. Crease the seam on the lap, turn the lap; baste down, entirely covering the joining, and stitch. Join the overlap piece to the front edge of the slash in the same manner. Adjust the overlap so that it will conceal the underlap and baste it in place. Stitch all around the overlap, following the shape of the point. At the top of the opening the stitching should cross the lap and catch through the underlap, securely holding the opening in correct position, as shown in Illustrations 157 and 158.

A continuous lap is often used to finish the slash at the cuff opening. This lap is made by sewing a straight strip of the material continuously along both edges of the slashed opening, the strip of material being the same width all its length, tapering the seam to almost nothing at top of slash. The other side is turned over and hemmed by hand or machine-stitched, to cover the first seam. When the lower edge of the sleeve is gathered, this lap is turned under at the front or overlapping edge of the opening and extended on the other side to form an underlap. (Illustration 159.)

Making and finishing the cuff—There are two sections for each cuff.

An interlining may be used in a cuff or not, depending on the degree of mannish effect desired in the garment. The interlining gives a cuff a more mannish look. It should be of a material about the same weight as the garment material, and is used to give a little more body to the cuff, but not to stiffen it. In many cases the material of the garment could be used for an interlining. In wash materials a soft cambric makes a good interlining.

If an interlining is used, baste it to the wrong side of one of the cuff sections. Then baste the second cuff section to the first with the right sides facing each other, stitching along the two ends and lower edge. Trim off the seam at the corners and turn the cuff right side out, making sure that the corners are as neat as possible. Baste along the seamed edges so that the cuff will be easy to handle in sewing it to the sleeve.

For a link cuff baste the upper edge of the outside, interlined section to the sleeve and overlap, but not to the underlap (Illustration 157); and in a lapped cuff, to the sleeve, overlap and underlap (Illustration 158). Then stitch. Turn the seam down and baste. Make a narrow turning on the inside of the cuff and baste it to position, covering the seam. Stitch around all the edges of the cuff from the outside. For convenience in handling it is better to turn the sleeve wrong side out before making this stitching.

In basting and sewing in sleeves hold the sleeve toward you so that the fulness can be distributed evenly. (Illustration 160.)

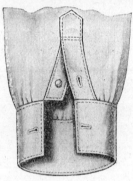

157—For a link closing

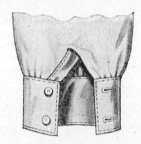

159—The continuous lap with the cuff attached

158—For a lapped closing

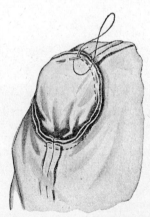

160—The correct method of basting or sewing a sleeve to the armhole

Belts and Casings

A belt may be cut double and the edges turned in toward each other, basted and stitched.

It may be cut in two sections, an outer section and an under section or lining, the edges turned in toward each other, basted and stitched.

It may be cut in two sections, an outer section and an under section, which may be laid with the right sides face to face and stitched together on both sides and across one end. It is then turned right side out and the open ends slip-stitched together.

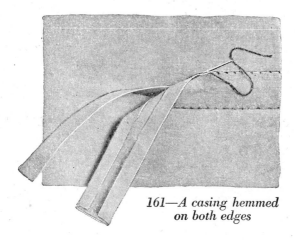

*161—A casing hemmed
on both edges*

A casing is used on a garment in places where it is necessary to have the fulness adjustable such as the waistline or top of an underslip, etc. An elastic or drawstring is run through the casing and is drawn up or let out as desired.

In some cases a casing is made by stitching a hem on each edge; in other cases it is applied to either the right or wrong side of a garment. This second form is a straight piece of material with its edges turned under as shown in Illustration 161. The width of the casing depends on the character of the garment and where it is used. For example, you would require a wider casing at the waistline of mohair or serge bloomers than at the waistline of a step-in. The casing can be made of the same material as the garment if it is suitable. In the case of mohair, serge or any other material that would make a clumsy casing you can use a piece of strong silk or lining material for the casing.

The casing is sewed flat to the garment at both edges either by hemming it (Illustration 161) or by machine-stitching.

Chapter XIV

POCKETS

Bound Pockets—Pockets with Welts—Patch Pockets

THE making and applying of pockets is a part of garment-making that home sewers sometimes fear to undertake, yet there is no real reason for this fear. Any one who is accurate in cutting, stitching and folding, and who uses the pressing-iron to secure clear-cut lines and edges, can make a pocket with all the smartness of finish that marks the best tailored garments.

In any Butterick Pattern that calls for a pocket, directions for making it are given on the Deltor, but a general acquaintance with the principal kinds of pockets used by tailors is often a help in remodeling, and the following methods of making the standard varieties of pockets may be adapted to this need by making the size, shape and variety fit the spot where the pocket is needed.

Bound Pockets

Hip Pocket

The pocket illustrated is the regulation hip pocket for men's trousers. The method of inserting it may be used in any other place where a bound pocket with a horizontal opening is required.

Mark with a row of basting stitches the line where the pocket opening is to come.

Cut the pocket from strong cotton or drill, making it about two inches wider than the opening and three inches more than twice as long as you want the finished pocket to be. Place one end on the inside of the garment with its edge ½ inch above the basting line and baste it to position. (Illustration 162.)

Cut a piece of the material for a facing. It should be about two inches wide and an inch longer than the line of basting that marks the pocket opening. Turn the garment to the right side and baste the facing, face down, with its center exactly over the basting line. (Illustration 163.)

Stitch across the ends and along the sides of this basting, keeping ⅛ of an inch away and making exact right angles at the corners. Tie the threads securely. (Illustration 163.)

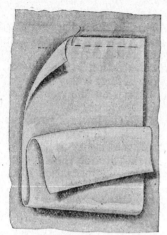

162—*Baste on the Pocket*

164—*Push in the facing*

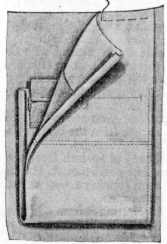

166—*Baste up the top*

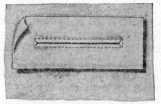

163—*Stitch on the facing and slash along the center*

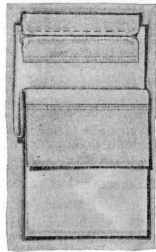

165—*Stitch one edge of each facing to the pocket*

167—*The finished pocket as it looks from the outside*

Hip Pocket
A Bound Pocket with a Horizontal Opening

Slash along the basting line through all thicknesses to within ³⁄₁₆ of an inch from each end. (Illustration 163.)   Make a diagonal cut from that point almost, but not quite, to the stitching line at each corner, forming a —< at each end.   Press the seams open.

Push the facing through the opening (Illustration 164) letting it form a binding ⅛ of an inch wide. This will form a tiny inverted plait at each end on the wrong side. Stitch, on the right side, along the line where the lower binding joins the garment.

Turn the garment wrong side up and stitch the lower edge of the facing to the pocket, but not to the garment. (Illustration 165.)

Cut another facing from the material, making it as long as the pocket is wide, and place it on the pocket section three inches from the unattached end. Stitch to position. (Illustration 165.) Turn the pocket up and baste.

Turn the garment to the right side and stitch along the upper edge of the binding, through all thicknesses. Illustration 166 shows this stitching from the wrong side.

Put crosswise stitches through the edges of the binding to hold them together until the garment is finished. (Illustration 167.)

Turn in the side edges of the pocket and stitch them close to the edge, also ¼ inch from the edge. Baste the upper edge along the top of the trousers. (Illustration 166.)

Stitch across at each end of the pocket to reinforce the opening. Finish each end with a bar tack. (Illustration 167.)

Bound Pocket with a Vertical Opening

The pocket illustrated is for the left side of a garment. For the right side, the arrangement would be reversed.

Run a line of basting to mark the pocket opening, letting it show plainly on both sides of the material.

Arrange a pocket section on the inside of the garment with the back edge extending one inch behind this line of basting (Illustration 168) and baste to position. Turn the garment right side up and baste a facing on the outside, face down, with the center over the basting line that marks the pocket opening.

Run a line of stitching through all thicknesses across the ends and along the sides, keeping it ⅛ of an inch from the basting line and being sure that the corners are exact right angles.

Slash along the basting line to within ³⁄₁₆ of an inch from each end, and make a cut diagonally from that point almost, but not quite, to the stitching line at each corner, forming a —< at each end. (Illustration 169.) Press the seams open.

Push the facing through to the inside, letting it form a binding ⅛ of an inch wide. (Illustration 170.) This will form a tiny inverted plait at each end on the wrong side. (Illustration 172.) Baste and press. Put stitches through the binding edges to hold

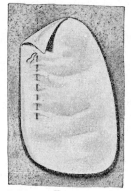

168 — Baste one pocket section inside

169—Stitch the facing, and slash

170—Push the facing inside

171—Hold the edges together with stitches

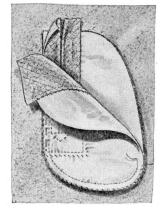

173—Finish the ends with arrowhead tacks

172—Adjust the inner section

A Bound Pocket with a Vertical Opening

them in shape until the garment is finished. (Illustration 171.)

Stitch the front edge of the opening through the seam that holds the binding to the garment and again ½ inch in front of the seam.

If the material is heavy, overhand the raw edges of the facing to the pocket section. If it is not heavy, turn the edge under ⅜ of an inch and fell to position. (Illustration 172.)

Arrange a facing of the material on the other pocket section as illustrated, so that it will lie under the pocket opening, and finish the raw edges in the same way the other section was finished. Lay this section on the one that is attached to the garment, with edges even and baste the back edge through the garment. (Illustration 172.)

Turn the garment to the outside and stitch along the seam and again ½ inch back of the seam.   Stitch the ends as illustrated, to form a triangle.   If desired, finish the ends with arrow-heads. (Illustration 173.)

Turn the garment to the inside.   Baste and stitch the sections together and overcast the edges.

Press the finished pocket from both the inside and outside of the garment.

Bound Pocket with a Curved Opening

Run a line of basting to mark the pocket opening, letting it show plainly on both sides of the material.

Arrange a pocket section on the inside of the garment with the upper edge ½ inch above this basting.   (Illustration 174.)

Arrange a facing, about five inches wide and shaped as illustrated (Illustration 175) face down on the outside, with the upper edge ¾ of an inch above the basting that marks the pocket opening.   Baste both to position.

Stitch across the ends and along the sides ⅛ of an inch from the line that marks the pocket opening.   Slash between the stitchings to within 3/16 of an inch from each end.   (Illustration 175.)   Make a cut from that point almost, but not quite, to the stitching at each corner, forming a ─< at each end of the slash.

Push the facing through to the inside, letting it form an ⅛-inch binding, and baste.   (Illustration 176.)   This will form a tiny inverted plait at each end on the wrong side.   (Illustration 177.)

Put cross-stitches through the binding edges to hold them in shape until the garment is finished.   (Illustration 176.)

Turn under the lower edge of the facing ⅜ of an inch and stitch twice to the pocket section but not to the garment; or, if the material is of a kind that does not fray, the raw edge may be over-handed to the pocket section.

Turn the garment to the right side and run a row of stitching through all thicknesses along the line where the lower binding joins the garment.

Arrange another facing on the other pocket section and finish the raw edges in the same manner as the section already attached. Baste the inner section to the outer, with the edges even.   Stitch the side and lower edges and overcast.   (Illustration 177.)

Turn the garment to the outside and run a row of stitching through all thicknesses along the line where the upper binding joins the garment.

Stitch across twice at each end to reinforce the pocket.   Finish the ends with bar tacks, if desired.

Press the finished pocket (Illustration 178) from both the inside and outside of the garment.

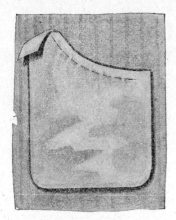

174—Baste a pocket section
on the inside

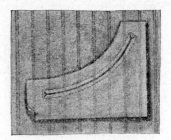

175—Stitch the facing outside, and slash

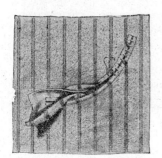

176—Push the facing
through the slash

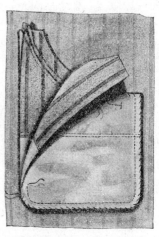

177—Join the inner section
to the outer one

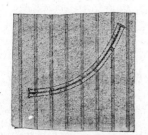

178—The finished pocket
from the outside

A Bound Pocket with a
Curved Opening

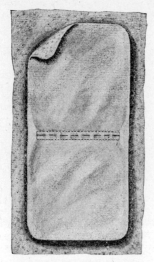

*179—Stitch the pocket
to the outside*

A Bound Pocket with
Binding and Pocket
Section in One Piece

*181—Put stitches across
the edges*

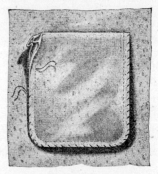

*182—Stitch the sections
together inside*

*180—Slash, and push the
pocket through*

*183—The pocket from
the outside*

Pocket with Binding and Pocket Section in One Piece

This method of making a bound pocket is for use when the material is light in weight and when you have enough of your garment material or of a contrasting material to make the pocket.

Run a line of basting to mark the pocket opening, letting it show plainly on both sides of the material.

Arrange the section on the outside of the garment with right sides together and the center of the section over the line of basting that marks the opening of the pocket. Baste to position. Stitch across the ends and each side of the line of basting, keeping $\frac{1}{8}$ of an inch from it on each side. (Illustration 179.) Slash along the basting line to within $\frac{3}{16}$ of an inch from each end. Make a diagonal cut from that point almost, but not quite, to the stitching line at each corner, forming a ➤ at each end. Press the seams open.

Push the pocket through to the inside, letting it form a binding $\frac{1}{8}$ of an inch wide on the right side. (Illustration 180.) This will form a tiny inverted plait at each end on the wrong side. Put crosswise stitches through the binding edges to hold them in shape until the garment is finished. (Illustration 181.) Run lines of stitching above and below the opening, along the lines where the upper and lower bindings join the garment. (Illustration 181.)

Turn to the inside of the garment and fold the upper section down. Baste and stitch the edges of the two pocket sections together, trimming off any unevenness. Overcast the edges. (Illustration 182.)

Press the finished pocket (Illustration 183) from both the inside and outside of the garment.

Pocket with In-and-Out Lap

Run a line of basting to mark the pocket opening, letting it show plainly on both sides of the material.

The lap must be finished completely before the pocket is begun. Cut the piece for the lap from the material of the garment, being careful to have the grain or stripe match the garment when the lap is laid on in the position it will take when the pocket is completed. (Illustration 188.) Stitch the lap and its lining with right sides together, then turn right side out and baste around the turned edges. Leave the finished edges soft or stitch close to the edge, according to the finish of the garment. Press. Baste along the top, leaving the edges raw and being careful to have the top, or outer, section a trifle easy.

Baste a pocket section on the inside of the garment, placing the top $\frac{1}{2}$ inch above the line of basting that marks the opening of the pocket. (Illustration 184.)

Turn the garment to the outside. Cut a facing of the material about two inches wide and long enough to extend one inch beyond each end of the basting line that marks the pocket opening. Lay this on the garment below the line for the opening and with its upper edge just touching this line. Baste and stitch $\frac{1}{8}$ of an inch below the edge. (Illustration 185.)

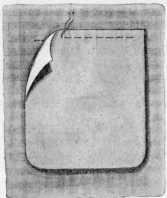

184—Baste one section
inside the garment

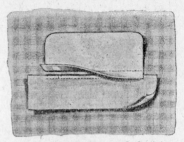

185—Stitch lap and facing
on the outside

186—Slash, and push the
facing through

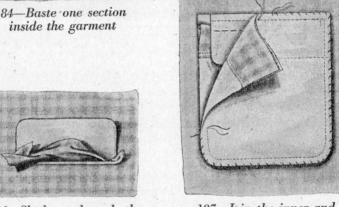

187—Join the inner and
outer sections

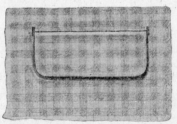

188—Finished Pocket from the outside

A Pocket with an In-and-Out Lap

Lay the lap right side down on the outside of the garment, with its finished edge upward and its raw edge extending ⅛ of an inch below the line of stitching that holds the facing to the garment. (Illustration 185.)

Stitch the lap to the garment ⅛ of an inch above the top of the facing.

Slash between the stitchings, being sure to turn the edge of the lap up out of the way. (Illustration 185.)

Press the seam of the facing open and push the facing through the opening, letting it form a binding ⅛ of an inch wide. (Illustration 186.) Baste and stitch along the line where the binding joins the garment. Turn the lap down and baste close to the upper edge.

Turn the garment to the inside and stitch the facing twice near the lower edge, stitching it to the pocket section but not to the garment. (Illustration 187.)

Push the lap through to the inside, with the raw edge upward and the lap downward, and baste to the garment just below the pocket opening. (Illustration 187.)

Face the inner pocket section with a piece of material about three inches wide, of the same kind used for the lap.

Place the inner pocket section over the outer, with the edges even, and baste along the upper edge. If the garment is finished with soft edges, blindstitch the top of the inner section to the garment. If the garment is finished with stitched edges, turn it to the right side and stitch through all thicknesses just above the line where the lap joins the garment, sew at each end to reenforce the opening.

Turn the garment wrong side out and stitch the pocket sections together. Overcast the edges. (Illustration 187.)

Finish the ends with bar tacks on the right side.

Pull out the basting that holds the pocket-lap and pull the lap out through the opening. (Illustration 188.)

Press the finished pocket from both the inside and outside of the garment.

Pocket Bound with Braid

Run a line of basting to mark the pocket opening, letting it show plainly on both sides of the material.

Baste a pocket section on the inside of the garment with the upper edge ¾ of an inch above this line of basting. (Illustration 189.)

Turn the garment to the outside and stitch along both sides of this line, keeping ⅛ of an inch away from it on each side. Tie the ends securely.

Slash along the basting line. If the material frays easily overcast the raw edges. (Illustration 190.)

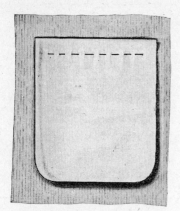

189—Baste one pocket section inside the garment

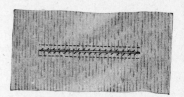

190—If the material frays easily, overcast the cut edges

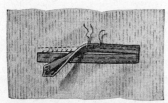

191—Slip the folded braid over the edges and stitch

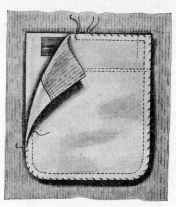

192—Stitch the pocket sections together and overcast the edges

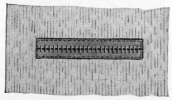

193—The finished pocket showing the crosswise stitches

A Pocket Bound with Braid

Cut two pieces of braid, slightly longer than the pocket opening. Turn in one end of each piece of braid and fold the braid in half lengthwise. Press lightly so that the fold will be marked. Slip the raw edges of the opening between the edges of the braid and baste, turning in the other ends of the braid and clipping the corners as necessary. Stitch the lower edge of the lower binding. (Illustration 191.)

Put crosswise stitches through the bound edges to hold them in shape until the garment is finished.   (Illustration 193.)

Arrange a facing of the material on the other pocket section and stitch the lower edge twice to position.   Place this section over the other with the upper edges even, and baste.   Turn the garment to the right side and stitch through all thicknesses along the line where the upper piece of braid joins the garment.

Turn the garment to the wrong side and stitch and overcast the edges of the pocket together.   (Illustration 192.)

Turn the garment to the right side and stitch along the turned-in edges of the braid at each end to reenforce the pocket opening, stitching through all thicknesses.   (Illustration 193.)

Press the finished pocket (Illustration 193) from both the inside and outside of the garment.

Pockets with Welts

Pocket with a Lined Welt

This method is to be used when the material of the garment is too heavy for a folded welt.

Run a line of basting to mark the opening of the pocket, letting the basting show plainly on both sides of the material.   If the pocket is to be cut through more than one thickness of material, baste around the marking so that the materials can not slip when the opening is cut.

Cut an interlining for the welt $3/8$ of an inch smaller at the top and ends than the welt pattern.   Turn the edges of the welt over on the interlining at the top and ends, mitering it neatly at the corners.   Baste and catch-stitch to position.   Stitch to match the rest of the garment and press carefully.

Lay the welt face down below the pocket line on the right side of the garment (Illustration 194) with the raw edge exactly even with the line of basting that marks the pocket opening.   Baste it in place.

The pocket is cut from the material that is used to line the garment.   Lay the inner section of the pocket face down on the right side of the garment, above the pocket line, with its edge close to the edge of the welt, and baste it in place.   (Illustration 194.)   Run a row of machine-stitching $1/4$ of an inch from each of these edges, and tie the threads securely.   Slash between the welt and the pocket section, following the basting line to within $3/16$ of an inch from each end.   Make a diagonal cut from that point almost, but not quite, to the stitching at each corner forming a —< at each end.   (Illustration 195.)

*194—Adjust the welt and
one pocket section*

*195—Sew the other pocket
section to the welt*

*196—The finished pocket
from the inside*

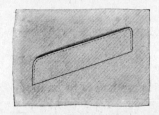

*197—The finished pocket
from the outside*

A Pocket with a
Lined Welt

Press the welt seam open and the seam of the pocket section upward. Catch-stitch the welt edge to the interlining. (Illustration 195.)

Push the pocket section through the opening. (Illustration 195.)

Turn under the upper edge of the outer pocket section ⅜ of an inch and fell it ⅛ of an inch from the top of the welt. (Illustration 195.) Fasten it to the other edge of the welt by putting a row of running stitches along the line of the seam that holds the welt to the garment, being sure that the stitches catch the seam but do not show through on the right side of the garment. (Illustration 195.)

Push this section through the opening. Turn the welt upward and baste it to position.

Turn the garment wrong side out and place a small piece of lining material at each end of the pocket to reenforce it. (Illustration 196.) Turn to the right side of the garment. Blind sew the ends of the welt to the garment, through the reenforcement, and again ¼ of an inch in from each end. Turn to the inside of the garment. Baste the pocket sections together, stitch around the sides and bottom and overcast the edges. (Illustration 196.)

Press the finished pocket (Illustrations 196 and 197) from both the inside and outside of the garment.

Pocket with Welt and Pocket Section in One Piece

This method is to be used when material is light in weight and you have enough to make the pocket and welt of the same material as the garment or of a contrasting material.

Run a line of basting to mark the opening of the pocket, letting the basting show plainly on both sides of the material.

Baste both pocket sections face down on the right side of the

199—Slash, and push the sections through

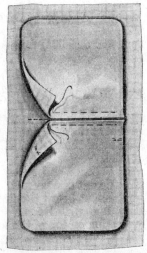

198—Baste both sections to the outside of the garment

201—The finished pocket from the inside

200—The finished pocket from the outside

A Pocket with Welt and Pocket Section in One Piece

garment, with the raw edges exactly even with the line of basting that marks the opening of the pocket. (Illustration 198.)

Run a row of machine-stitching $\frac{3}{8}$ of an inch from each edge, leaving $\frac{3}{4}$ of an inch between stitchings, and tie the threads securely.

Slash along the basted line to within $\frac{3}{16}$ of an inch of each end. Make a cut diagonally from that point almost, but not quite, to the stitching line at each corner, forming a ─< at each end. Turn under the little triangle of material thus formed at each end of the pocket opening.

Push the pocket sections through the slash, creasing the lower section at indicating tailors' tacks to form a welt. (Illustration 199.)

Press down the seam at the lower edge of the opening, and press up the seam at the upper edge of the opening. Blindstitch along the seam at the lower edge to form the welt. Sew the ends of the welt to position. (Illustration 200.)

Stitch the pocket sections together and overcast the edges. (Illustration 201.)

Press the finished pocket (Illustrations 200 and 201) from both the inside and outside of the garment.

Pocket with a Folded Welt

This method is to be used when the material is light in weight but you have not enough to make the pocket of the material.

Run a line of basting to mark the opening of the pocket, letting it show plainly on both sides of the material.

Fold the welt in half, wrong side out. Baste and stitch the ends. (Illustration 202.) Turn it right side out and press it.

Lay the welt on the right side of the garment below the line of bastings that marks the pocket opening, and with its raw edge along this line. Place the outer pocket section on top of the welt, with edges even, and baste them to position. (Illustration 203.)

Lay the inner pocket section above the line that marks the opening, on the right side of the garment, with its edge exactly even with this line. (Illustration 203.) Put a row of stitching $\frac{1}{4}$ of an inch from each edge and tie the ends of the threads securely.

Slash along the pocket opening line to within $\frac{3}{16}$ of an inch from each end. Make a diagonal cut from that point almost, but not quite, to the stitching line, making a ─< at each end.

Push both pocket sections through the slash. (Illustration 204.) Turn the welt up and blindstitch the ends to position. (Illustration 205.) Stitch the pocket sections together and overcast the edges. (Illustration 206.) Press the finished pocket from both the inside and outside of the garment.

202—Fold the welt, wrong side out and baste the ends

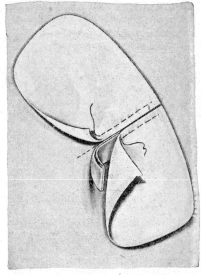

203—Lay the welt and pocket sections on the outside of the garment

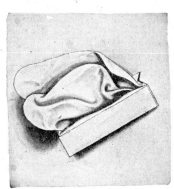

204—Slash, and push the pocket sections to the inside

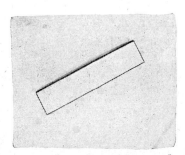

205—Turn the welt upward and blindstitch it to position

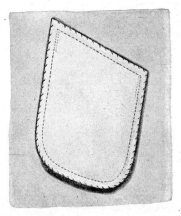

206—Stitch the pocket sections together and overcast the edges

A Pocket with a Folded Welt

Patch Pockets

Pocket with Outside Facing

Place the facing under the pocket with the right side of the material upward in both pieces. (Illustration 207.) Baste and stitch a seam across the top. Press the seam open. Turn the facing to the outside of the pocket and turn under the lower edge of the facing ⅜ of an inch. Stitch through both facing and pocket close to the upper and lower edges of the facing. (Illustration 208.)

Turn under the sides and bottom of the pocket, with the facing stitched to it, ⅜ of an inch; baste, press and place on garment. Baste to position and stitch close to the edge around the sides and bottom. (Illustration 209.) Turn the garment to the inside and sew the upper side edges of the pocket invisibly to the garment, to reinforce the pocket. Press the finished pocket from both the inside and outside of the garment.

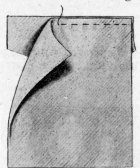

207—Place the facing under the pocket

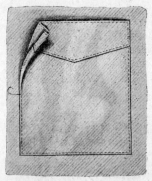

209—Stitch the pocket to the garment around the sides and bottom

208—Stitch close to the edges of the facing

A Patch Pocket with an Outside Facing

A Patch Pocket with a Lap

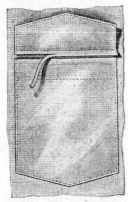

210—Stitch the sections
of the lap together

211—Turn in the edges
of the pocket

212—Stitch the lap
above the pocket

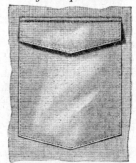

213—Turn down the
lap and stitch

Patch Pocket with a Lap

Arrange the sections for the lap with the right sides together, baste, and stitch $\frac{3}{8}$ of an inch from the side and lower edges. (Illustration 210.) Clip the corners. Turn right side out, baste, press, and stitch close to the edge.

Turn under $\frac{3}{8}$ of an inch around the sides and bottom of the pocket and baste. Turn the hem allowed at the top and stitch. (Illustration 211.) Place the pocket on the garment and stitch close to the side and lower edges. (Illustration 212.)

Turn the garment to the inside and sew the upper side edges of the pocket invisibly to the garment, to reinforce it.

Place the lap above the pocket, right side down, with the raw edge even with the upper edge of the pocket, and stitch it $\frac{3}{8}$ of an inch above its edge. (Illustration 212.) Trim off the edge full $\frac{1}{8}$ inch; turn the lap down and stitch it $\frac{1}{4}$ of an inch from the top. (Illustration 213.)

Press the pocket from both the inside and outside of the garment.

Chapter XV

PLACKETS

Simple Placket at a Seam of a Skirt—Simple Placket Where There Is No
Strain—Continuous Lap Placket—Underwear Plackets

PLACKETS for skirts require neat workmanship. Great
care must be taken in handling the edges of the opening.
If the outer edge becomes stretched, it will bulge when the
skirt is on the figure—a defect you have probably noticed on other
women. Hooks and eyes and snaps (pages 152-155) should be
placed sufficiently close together to prevent the skirt from gaping.
Any stitching that shows through on the outside should be done
evenly and with a suitable stitch and tension. Otherwise the
placket will have a careless appearance.

A placket opening should be deep enough to slip over the head
easily. The design of the skirt regulates the position and finish
of the placket.

Simple placket at a seam of a skirt—Face the right side of the
opening with silk and stitch the edge. Sew an underlap of material an inch and a half wide, finished, to the left side of the opening and line this underlap with silk. Sew on snaps. Hooks used
with eyes, blind loops or bar eyes, make a strong fastening for
the top of a skirt. (Illustration 214.)

Simple placket where there is no strain—Illustration 215 shows a
simple finish for a placket which may be used for a silk skirt that
has fulness at the top so that no strain comes on the placket. The
overlapping edge is finished with a facing and the under edge with
an underlap. The facing can be machine-stitched or finished
invisibly by hand according to the finish of the skirt. Snaps
may be used for the closing since there is no strain. The snaps
should be placed about two inches apart.

Continuous lap placket—A placket such as is made for light-
weight silk and cotton dresses and underwear is shown in Illustration 216. This placket is used on dresses when outside sewing

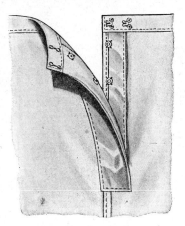

214—A simple placket at a seam of a skirt, inside view

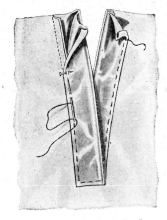

215—A simple placket where there is no strain

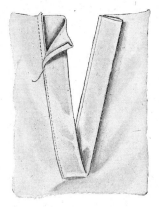

216—Inside view of a continuous lap placket used on a slash

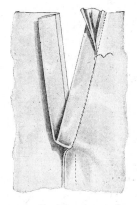

217—Inside view of a continuous lap placket closing used at a seam

would be an objection; also on dresses that have to visit the laundry. Use a strip twice the length of the opening and twice the width of the finished underlap plus ⅜ inch on each edge for a seam.

Lay the lap along the edge of the opening with the right side of both lap and skirt together and baste them in a narrow seam. (Illustration 216.) Run it almost to a point at the lower end of the opening. Turn the free edge under and hem it close to the sewing.

When this strip or lap is applied above a seam of a skirt, it is set back an eighth of an inch from the stitching of the seam. (Illustration 217.) One side is extended out to form the underlap, and the other side is turned under on an even line with the stitching of the seam.

In transparent fabrics such as chiffon, etc., which are not sent to the laundry, the skirt placket should be made as inconspicuous as possible. Don't face the placket edges, as the seams would show. Turn a hem and overcast the loose edges with a fine thread so that they will show as little as possible. These materials as a rule are made in soft styles where there is no strain on the placket edges. Snaps can be used for the closing, as few of them and as small as will hold the placket. Use no other sewing on the placket than the sewing for the snaps.

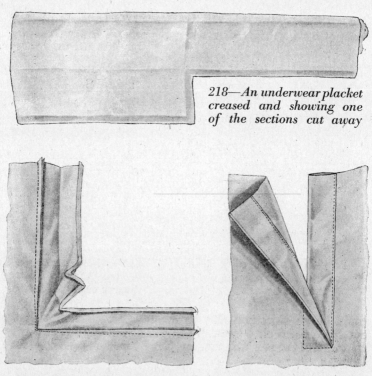

218—An underwear placket creased and showing one of the sections cut away

219—The placket with its long side stitched to the slash and its edges turned

220—The finished placket showing stitching on both the inside and outside

Underwear Plackets

Underwear plackets are made in the following manner: If there is no seam, cut the opening in the garment the desired length. It should be long enough to slip easily over the head. Cut for a lap a strip of material lengthwise of the goods. It should be twice the length of the placket opening and twice the width of the finished underlap plus ⅜ of an inch on each edge for a seam. Fold the ends together and crease through center; open and fold the sides together and crease. Cut out one section to within a small seam of the crease as shown in Illustration 218.

Baste the long straight edge of the lap to both edges of the opening, making a narrow seam. Run it almost to a point at the lower end of the opening. (Illustration 219.) Make a narrow turning on the three edges of both the narrow and the wide part of the lap. Double the wide part back (Illustration 219), baste the edge over the line of sewing, and hem it. This forms the underlap. Turn the narrow part back on the line of sewing, baste the free edge to the garment to form a facing, and stitch. The end of the underlap is turned under, basted and stitched across. The finished closing is shown in Illustration 220. This placket has an outside row of stitching. It is usually employed for the closing of drawers, petticoats, etc.

Chapter XVI

BUTTONHOLES, EYELETS, BUTTONS, SNAPS, HOOKS AND EYES AND BLIND LOOPS

Barred Buttonhole—Round-End Buttonhole—Tailors' Buttonhole—Eyelets—
Bound Buttonhole—Simulated Buttonhole—Loop Buttonhole—Sewing on
Buttons—Link Buttons—Covering Button-Molds—Sewing on Hooks and Eyes
—Blind Loops—Bar Eyes—Buttonholed Rings—Sewing on Snaps

A WELL-MADE garment that is otherwise perfect may be greatly injured in appearance by badly made buttonholes. They should always be properly spaced and marked before they are cut. Mark the position for the top and bottom buttonholes, and divide the distance between into the desired number of spaces. Cut the slit on the thread of the goods, if possible, and make it large enough to allow the button to slip through easily, as a properly made buttonhole becomes tighter after it is worked.

With the buttonhole scissors carefully test the length for the slit and make a clean cut with one movement of the scissors.

Buttonholes are strengthened with strands of thread to prevent the edges from stretching. Bring the needle up at one end and, allowing the thread to lie along the edge of the cut on the right side of the material, stick down at the opposite end. Do the same on the other side of the cut and stick down opposite the first stitch, with a stitch across the end to fasten the thread.((Illustration 223.)

If the material is inclined to fray, or when working a buttonhole in a coat where interlining is used and there is danger of the material slipping so the interlining will show, overcast the edges before working the buttonholes. (Illustration 224.)

To make the stitch, place the buttonhole over the forefinger of the left hand, holding it in position with the thumb and second finger as shown in Illustration 221. Begin to work the buttonhole close to the corner or starting-point. Insert the needle and, while it is pointing toward you, bring the double thread as it hangs from the eye of the needle around to the left and under the needle. Draw the needle through the loop, letting the thread form a purl exactly on the edge of the slip.

142

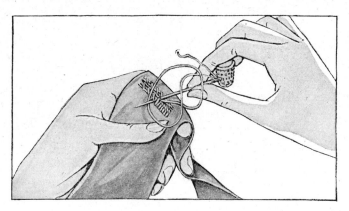

*221—The position of the needle and thread
in the making of a buttonhole-stitch*

The buttonhole with a bar at both ends. (Illustration 225.) Continue these stitches to the opposite end, being careful to take them the same depth and close together. Now pass the needle up and down through the goods until two or three threads cross the end of the slit quite close to the buttonhole-stitches, thus forming a bar tack. At the end turn the work around so that the bar end is toward you and make several buttonhole-stitches over the bar tack and through the material. Work the other side of the buttonhole and the second bar.

The round-end buttonhole—Illustration 226 shows this buttonhole. Begin the buttonhole-stitch as in the buttonhole with bars at both ends, working down one side. When the outer end is reached, take the stitches on a slant, inserting the needle each time at a little different angle until the end is rounded. Continue the work on the other side. Finish the inner end with a bar tack.

The tailors' or eyelet buttonhole is used for garments of heavy cloth, as the round end or eyelet provides a resting-place for the shank of the button or the stitches holding the button. Baste around the line to be cut so that the material will not slip, and cut the slit the desired length. At the outer end cut a small ≺ as shown in Illustration 222 and push a stiletto through to shape it as shown in Illustration 224.

After cutting, strand the buttonhole so that the worked edge will be firm and distinct. This may be done with two threads of twist. Tailors follow the plan of using a cord formed of several strands of buttonhole twist or linen thread twisted together, or a gimp cord. An end of this cord or thread is secured at the inner end of the buttonhole between the fabrics, and the other end is fastened to the knee or some convenient place and kept taut by a slight strain upon the work as it is held in the hand. By this strain the cord is kept straight and in position just back of the edge of the buttonhole.

Work the stitches over the cord by the usual movements. After

222—The cut for a tailors' buttonhole

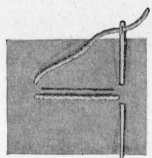

223—Correct method of making strands

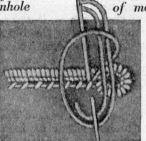

224—A tailors' buttonhole

225—The buttonhole with bars at both ends

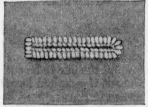

226—A round-end buttonhole with one end barred

each stitch is drawn down, pick the loose twist up firmly by the thumb and forefinger quite near the stitch, and make two or three circular twisting movements so that the loop formed will settle securely and neatly into its proper position.   Be careful to complete each stitch with uniform movements.   When the eyelet is reached, adjust the work so that the stitches may be made at the proper slant.   The stitches should radiate from the eyelet as the spokes do in a wheel.   (Illustration 224.)

The inner end of an eyelet buttonhole may be bar-tacked. Sometimes the bars are simply worked with an over-and-over stitch. This is done by passing the needle up through the fabric at one side of the bar and down through it at the other side until the bars are entirely covered with these stitches and the stays look like a fine cord.   After the buttonholes are worked, baste their edges together by an over-and-over stitch made by pushing the needle up and down over the edges just back of the stitches.   Then press them under a dampened cloth.   In fact, all buttonholes should be pressed if the goods will permit.   Before they are dry, push a stiletto up vigorously through each eyelet until the opening becomes perfectly round and the stitches around its edges are regular and distinct. When the bastings are removed, the buttonholes will be symmetrical in appearance.

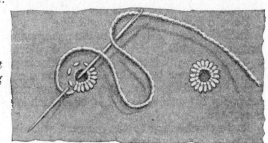

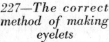

227—The correct method of making eyelets

Eyelets

Eyelets are holes made and worked in a garment to hold a cord or lingerie ribbon or the shanks of buttons that are detached for laundering.   The method of making them is shown in Illustration 227.   Pierce the eyelet-hole with a stiletto.   Make running stitches around the circle, place the hole over the forefinger of the left hand and buttonhole the edge, covering the running stitches.   Work from right to left, as illustrated.

Sometimes in lingerie the eyelets are elongated to take a wide ribbon.   This is done by snipping the hole very slightly on two opposite sides before making the running stitches.   For this kind of eyelet it is best to overcast the edge before working the buttonhole-stitch.

Bound Buttonholes

The bound buttonhole can be used on garments of wool, silk, linen, cotton or mixed materials. It gives a finished look to a coat or dress and is particularly effective when the binding is in a contrasting color, though the binding is frequently of the same material as the garment.

There are two ways of binding a buttonhole.

In either case, the position and length of the buttonhole should be marked on the garment with colored thread. (Illustration 228.)

When used on a garment which is not to be faced, where the wrong side of buttonholing is likely to show and must look the same as the outside, use for binding a bias strip of material $1\frac{5}{8}$ inch wide and $\frac{1}{4}$ inch longer than the finished buttonhole. Baste the binding to the garment with its center lying along the buttonhole mark and right sides together. Sew or stitch one-eighth of an inch from each side of the buttonhole mark and across the ends. (Illustration 229.)

Turn in the outer edges of binding one-eighth of an inch and press them flat. (Illustration 230.) Cut the buttonhole through the center, along the line marked by the basting (now covered by the stitched-on binding), cutting through both garment and binding almost to the stitching but not through it.

Be sure to cut a clean, straight line.

Push the binding through to the wrong side of the garment (Illustration 231) and slip-stitch it to position along the sewing line of the outside. Slip-stitch the ends of the binding so they will not fray.

When a bound buttonhole is used on a garment which is to be faced, or where the wrong side will not show, use for binding a bias strip $1\frac{3}{4}$ inch wide and $\frac{3}{4}$ of an inch longer than the finished buttonhole.

Baste the binding to the garment with its center at the mark and right sides together. Sew or stitch one-eighth of an inch from each side of the buttonhole mark and across the ends.

Cut the buttonhole on the mark, cutting the corners diagonally almost to the stitching. (Illustration 232.)

Push the binding through to the wrong side of the garment (Illustration 233) laying the fulness at the ends in a box plait. (Illustration 234.) Fasten the plaits with a few overhand stitches and sew the binding to position along the sewing line of the outside, but do not turn the edges under. Press well.

If the garment has a facing, baste it flat about an inch from the buttonhole. Cut a straight line in the lining at the buttonhole. Turn in the edges of the facing and slip-stitch to the binding.

Bound slashes—Slashes to run tie, belt, etc., through are finished the same as a bound buttonhole.

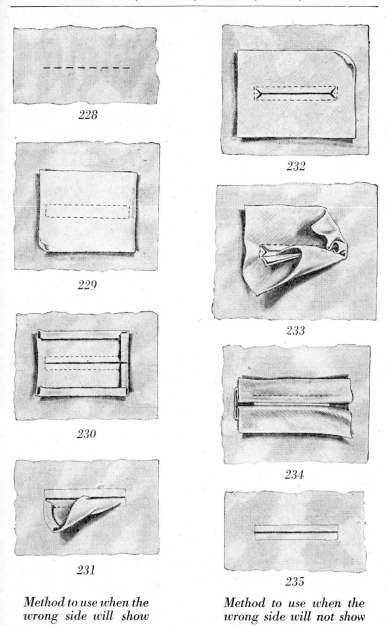

228

229

230

231

232

233

234

235

Method to use when the
wrong side will show

Method to use when the
wrong side will not show

Two Ways of Making Bound Buttonholes

A Simulated Buttonhole

This is made of a finished bias piping folded in half crosswise. The folded end is tacked to the material and the raw edges of the other end are pushed through to the wrong side of the material with a stiletto and tacked with a few stitches. (Illustration 236.)

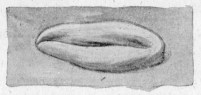

236—A simulated buttonhole

Loops

A loop buttonhole is made of a strip of finished bias piping with or without a cord inserted in it or of braid or cord. The strip should be long enough to make a loop that will slip easily over the button after the two raw ends of the loop are tacked together. These ends may be tacked to the back of a button (Illustration 237), or sewed between an edge and its facing (Illustration 238), or sewed to an edge before it is bound (Illustration 239), depending on the style effect required.

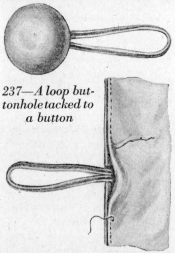

*237—A loop but-
tonhole tacked to
a button*

*238—A loop buttonhole sewed
between an edge and its facing*

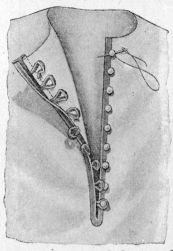

*239—Loop buttonholes sewed
to an edge before it is bound*

A worked loop buttonhole is used for fastening sleeves at the wrist and for closings for blouses, dresses, etc.   Use three or four threads of buttonhole twist or thread of the desired length and buttonhole closely over them.   (Illustration 240.)

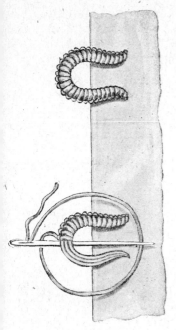

240—*Worked loop buttonholes*

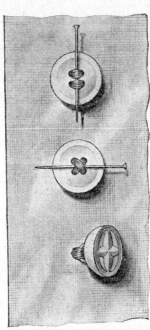

241—*Three ways of sewing on buttons*

Sewing on Buttons

Methods of sewing on buttons are shown in Illustration 241. Always use a coarse single thread in preference to a fine double one. In placing buttons in position lap the edges of the garment and push a pin through at the outer end of the buttonhole.   This will bring the button exactly opposite the buttonhole.   Make a knot in the thread, push the needle through from the right side so that the knot will be directly under the button.   Place the button in position.   For the method shown in the middle button in the illustration, bring the thread up through a hole and down through the hole diagonally opposite.   Place a pin under the thread on top of the button, in order to keep the thread loose, and make a cross-stitch through the remaining holes.

Repeat the stitches until the button is securely fastened. Remove the pin, draw the button away from the material as far as possible and wind the working thread tightly several times around the threads between the button and the material, thus forming a thread shank for the button. If a button is too closely sewed to the garment, it will not have room to rest easily in the buttonhole and will crowd the latter out of shape and make the spacing seem irregular. The loose sewing and the winding increase the durability of the work and lessen the strain on the button.

The button at the top of the illustration shows another way of sewing on a button in which the stitches are not crossed. This method is used in dress and coat making, as the stitches are considered more ornamental. The third illustration shows the method of sewing on a shank button. Make the stitches parallel with the edge when sewing on this button so that the strain will come on the shank.

In sewing buttons on coats, sew them through the coat and interlining but not through the lining or facing.

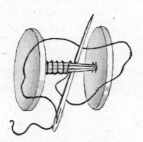 

242—*Buttons linked by strands of thread*   243—*Buttons linked by a fold of material*

Link Buttons

Link buttons are used to close the front of a dress or coat and to close cuffs and sleeves. They can be made in two ways. The first is to join together two buttons with four or five threads of twist, length desired, buttonhole across threads.

The second method is to cut a fold of material about two inches long, turn in the ends and slip-stitch. Tack buttons to the ends of the fold.

Covering Button-Molds

If the covering material is light weight, cut a thin piece of sheet wadding the shape of the mold but about 1/8 of an inch smaller all around. Place it on top of the mold.

Cut another piece of sheet wadding a little larger than the mold and place it over the mold on the first piece of wadding. Draw it up on the under side of the mold with a few crosswise stitches to make it lie flat.   If the outside material is heavy, the wadding may be omitted.

For the covering cut a piece of the outside material the same shape as the mold, and a little larger but not large enough to quite come together on the under side.   If it comes together, the button will be bunchy and clumsy.

Gather the cover about one-eighth of an inch from the edge with fine running stitches (Illustration 244) and lay it over the padded side of the mold.   Draw up the gathering-thread.   The gathering must be smooth and tight over the mold without any folds or wrinkles, especially at the edges.   A few stitches across the back will hold it.

If the button is to be used to fasten a garment, the back should be lined with a piece of the covering material.   Cut the lining the size of the mold and the same shape.   Turn the edges in and fell it neatly to the back of the button.   (Illustration 244.)   Put the facing on the back of the button so that it is slightly full.   This fulness serves as a shank.   If a button-mold is covered with heavy cloth,

244—Various steps in covering a button-mold

the lining should be of satin or some other thin material in the same color, for the cloth would be too bulky.

If the button is to be used as a trimming, the lining may be omitted.

For molds which have a hole in the center and which are covered with material that is not too heavy the covering may be cut large enough to cover the mold with just as much material in the back as can be forced into the hole with one's needle.

Sewing on Hooks and Eyes

Before sewing hooks and eyes on a lining, stitch each edge of the closing one-eighth of an inch back from the fold edge and again three-eighths of an inch from the first stitching as shown in Illustration 245. This gives a firm edge.

Pin the closing edges together with the upper and lower ends even. Place a tape measure along one edge and with pins mark the position for the hooks and eyes. For a waist they should be one and one-quarter inch apart. Place the hook well inside the edge and sew through the two rings and over the end of the bill. (Illustration 245.) This last sewing should be one-quarter of an inch from the edge of the garment.

In sewing on the eyes let the eye extend just far enough beyond the edge to fasten easily. (Illustration 245.) Sew the eye through the two rings and at the edge of the garment.

Sew them securely, for the sewing will give a little if there is any strain on the closing.

Be careful in sewing the hooks and eyes on the second side of the closing to have them exactly opposite the eyes and hooks on the first side.

After the hooks and eyes are sewed on, turn back the edge of the hem or facing and hem the folded edge by hand to the row of stitching near the edge of the closing (Illustration 245), covering the sewing of the hooks and eyes.

Blind Loops

These are used on garments fastened with hooks and eyes, to take the place of the eyes. The process of making them is shown in Illustration 246. Mark the position of the loop opposite the hook, knot the thread and bring the needle up through the material. Make a bar tack the desired length (Illustration 246) by taking three or more stitches one over the other. Working from left to right, hold the thread down with the left thumb, and insert the needle, eye foremost, under the bar and over the thread. (Illustration 246.)   The use of the blunt end of the needle facilitates the work.   Draw the thread up, letting the purl come to the lower edge of the loop.   Repeat the stitches, covering the entire bar tack, and fasten on the wrong side.   Sometimes the bar tacks are made in the form of a cross-stitch.

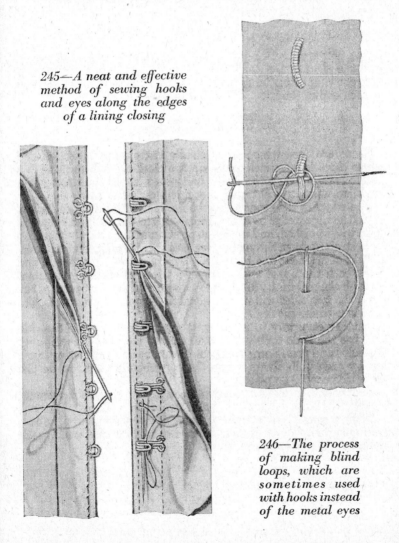

245—*A neat and effective method of sewing hooks and eyes along the edges of a lining closing*

246—*The process of making blind loops, which are sometimes used with hooks instead of the metal eyes*

Buttonholed Rings

Brass and celluloid rings are sometimes used in place of eyes.
They are also used to lace ribbon through. Cover the ring with
buttonhole-stitches, using the same method as for blind loops.
(Illustration 247.) Buttonhole the ring to the garment at mark
for it, inserting the point of the needle instead of the eye end.
(Illustration 248.) Use buttonhole twist or heavy thread.

Bar Eyes

Bar eyes are used on garments fastened with hooks and eyes to
take the place of the usual eyes when there is danger of the usual
eyes showing after the garment is closed. Sew through the ring
at each end of the bar. (Illustration 249.)

Sewing on Snaps

Snaps are used where an especially flat closing is desired and
where there is not much strain on the closing. Where there is a
decided strain, as on the inside belt of a skirt or the closing of a
brassière, snaps will not hold as securely as hooks and eyes.

The edges of the closing may be finished with a hem or facing.
Place the upper edge over the under edge in the position they will
be in when finished, and mark the position of the snaps by running
a pin straight down through both edges about one-quarter or three-
eighths of an inch from the edge. Separate the edges a little and
mark both the upper and under edges just where the pin passes
through the material. If you use these marks for the center of the
snap, the two sides will match exactly. The heaviest part of the
snap is used for the under part.

Another easy way to make snaps match is to sew on the side
that has the little bulb first. Rub tailors' chalk or a pencil over
the bulbs and press down evenly on the other side. The tiny mark
left by each bulb shows where the corresponding section on the
other side should be placed.

Several stitches should be taken through each of the holes around
the edge of the snap, enough to hold it securely. (Illustration 250.)

When a snap is sewed through one thickness of material, as at a
trimming line, ribbon binding or tape should be used underneath
the material to relieve the strain.

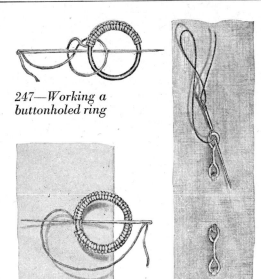

247—*Working a buttonholed ring*

248—*Attaching a buttonholed ring*

249—*Sewing on bar eyes*

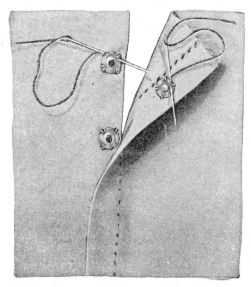

250—*Sewing snaps on a skirt placket*

Chapter XVII

TUCKS AND PLAITS

Tucks—Nun's Tucks—Curved Tucks—Cross-Tucking—Laying Plaits—Stitching Plaits—Cutting Away Plaits in Heavy Material

TUCKS should be marked with a measure so that they will be of even width. When the tucking attachment of the machine is used, it gages and marks the tucks in any material that will hold a crease.

Nun's tucks are wide tucks usually two inches or more in width. The method of making all tucks is the same more or less, but the wider the tucks, the greater the difficulty in keeping the tucks and the distance between them even, especially when they are used at the bottom of a circular skirt. In such a case the tucks must be marked and basted before the stitching is done.

There are gages obtainable, of various materials such as metal, wood or celluloid, with the inches plainly marked and in some cases notched on one side; or a gage can be cut from stiff cardboard with the notches placed just where desired.

To make a gage, cut a piece of cardboard, and from the end measure down the width of the first tuck, making a slash and a bias cut to meet the slash. (Illustration 251.) Make a second cut as shown in the illustration, allowing for the space between tucks and for the second tuck.

It is usually quicker and more accurate to make a gage of this sort in measuring short spaces, such as hems, tucks and the spaces between them, than to use a ruler or tape measure, as sometimes the eye becomes confused at the small marks on the measure, and mistakes are made that will prove quite serious.

Curved tucks—Curved tucks are sewed on a curved line which makes the under side fuller than the upper side. Mark the edge of the tuck with tailors' tacks (pages 91-92) or pins, fold the material on this mark and baste quite close to the edge. (Illustration 252.) Mark the depth of the tuck from this edge, using a gage to keep the tuck an even width, and baste. In sewing the tuck the extra fulness must be eased on the under side of the tuck as you sew. Be careful to distribute this fulness evenly so that it does not fall in bunches or draw the edge of the tuck out of place.

156

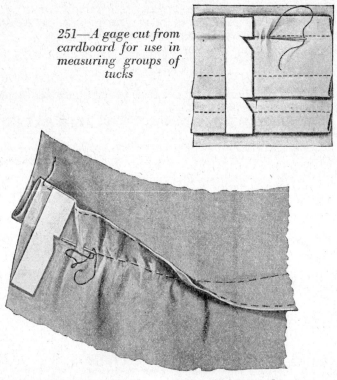

251—*A gage cut from cardboard for use in measuring groups of tucks*

252—*A gage used in measuring a wide curved tuck*

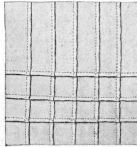

253—*Cross-tucking with all the tucks the same width and with the same distance between tucks*

Cross-tucking is an effective trimming for children's clothes, blouses, dresses, etc. All tucks running in one direction should be made first. The cross-tucks may be the same size and placed the same distance apart as the first tucks, so that when the tucks and cross-tucks are finished they will form perfect squares (Illustration 253), or they may be of graduated sizes or used in groups to give the desired effect.   Cross-tucks may be of various sizes, but pin-tucks placed about an inch apart (measuring from the sewing of one tuck to the edge of the next) are particularly dainty.

Plaits

In laying plaits in a garment it is generally advisable to lay them before the seams are joined.

Be careful to get the plaits even, without any draw, especially when the edges come bias.

As each plait is flattened, it should be basted a little distance from the fold edge, as shown in Illustration 254, to keep it in shape.

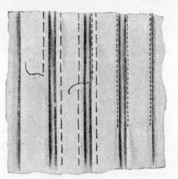

254—A plaited skirt show-
ing basting and stitching

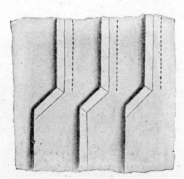

255—A plaited skirt of heavy
material with the underlap-
ing material cut away from
the stitched part

256—Plaits stitched part
way with the threads pulled
through to the wrong side
and tied

This will be found a great convenience later in working on the garment.

In stitching plaits it is best to leave at least one seam of the garment open, and if it is a skirt, remove it from the belt or camisole, for the work can be more easily handled under the machine if it is open and flat. After stitching the plaits as desired, baste and stitch the seam, and, if it is a skirt, put it on the belt or camisole and try the skirt on to get the correct length. A hem is generally better than a facing for the bottom of a plaited skirt or dress, because the seam at the lower edge would be too bulky. Press the plaits.

When a plaited skirt is made of heavy material or is lapped very much at the waist in fitting, it may be made less bulky by cutting away the surplus material after the plaits are stitched. The under-lapping material is cut away to within an inch or so of where the stitching finishes. (Illustration 255.) From that point it is cut across the top of the plait. The raw edges left in this way are bound with a bias strip of lining or with ribbon seam binding, that will finish across the top of each plait (Illustration 255) except where the seams that join the breadths form the inner fold of a plait. In that case the binding will continue down the raw edges of that seam to the bottom of the skirt.

In cases where tucks or plaits are not stitched the entire length, the thread-ends on the under side must be securely tied, as shown in Illustration 256.

Chapter XVIII

BIAS TRIMMINGS

Bias Bindings, Double and Single—Binding with Braid or Ribbon—Binding with Bias-Fold Tape—Binding a Scalloped Edge in Sheer Material—Piping—Cording—Cord Motifs—Corded Tucks—Cord Piping—Tie with Ball Trimming —Bands, Folds and Straps—The Unlined Fold—The Lined Fold—The Piped Fold—Double Folds—Milliners' Folds—Tailors' Straps—Tie for Sailor Blouse

BIAS bindings make attractive finishes either in same or in a contrasting material or color. They are obtainable in many materials and widths, and wherever a ready-made binding can be used it is a saving of time to use it. Where they must match the garment, however, they must of course be cut from the same material and must be cut on a true bias. (See page 61.)

Bias bindings may be single or double. In wools, heavy cottons or linens use a single binding, as a double binding of these materials would be too bulky. Double binding is better in the lighter-weight materials, as it is easier to handle.

Always cut away the seam allowance from edges to be bound.

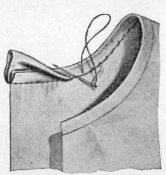

257—Double bind-
ing around a neck

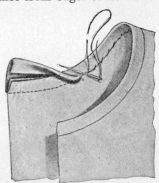

258—Single bind-
ing around a neck

Double binding—Cut bias strips of the material a trifle more than *four times* the width the finished binding is to be, plus an allowance for a seam on each edge. Join the strips, if necessary (page 62), and press the seams open. Fold the finished strip through the center and press. Stitch or sew the raw edges to the outside of the edge that is to be bound, the seam's width from the edge, with the binding toward you. Roll to the inside and fell the folded edge to the line of sewing that holds the outside. (Illustration 257.) Be careful not to let the bias strips twist.

Single binding—Cut bias strips *twice* the width of the finished binding, plus allowance for a seam on each edge. Stitch or sew one edge to the outside, the seam's width from the edge, with the binding toward you. Roll to the inside. Turn in the edge the width of the seam allowance and fell it to the line of sewing that holds the outside. (Illustration 258.) Be careful not to let the bias strips twist.

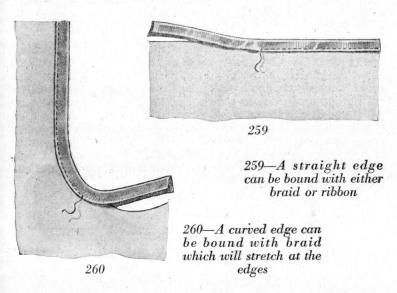

259

259—A straight edge can be bound with either braid or ribbon

260—A curved edge can be bound with braid which will stretch at the edges

260

Binding with braid or ribbon—Fold the braid or ribbon through the center and press. Slip the material between the edges of the braid or ribbon and baste and stitch. Dampening braid at the ends makes it easier to handle. Braid can be stretched around curves the same as any of the bias trimmings, but ribbon of course, can not.

Binding with bias-fold tape—There are two ways of binding with bias-fold tape. Sew or stitch one edge of the tape to the outside along the crease in the tape with the tape toward you. Roll to the inside and fell the folded edge to the line of sewing that holds the outside. (Illustration 261.) Or, for a quick finish, it may be put on by the same method as braid or ribbon. (Illustration 262.)

261—One method of binding with bias - fold tape

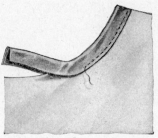

262—Another way to bind with bias-fold tape

Binding a scalloped edge in sheer material—To prevent stretching and to retain the original shaping of the scallops, mark the outline of pattern on tissue-paper about two inches wider than the deepest part of the scallops, and baste the scalloped edge of the material to the outline on the tissue-paper. (Illustration 263.) Baste and stitch a binding of the material, through the paper, to the edge that is to be bound, binding toward you, stretching the binding at the points of the scallops. (Illustration 264.) Tear the paper away from the edge, roll the binding to the inside, lay the fulness at each point in a tiny plait or miter and fell the folded edge to position. (Illustration 265.)

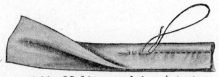

266—Making a plain piping

Piping

Piping is a finish which is much used in dressmaking. It is easy to use and gives an opportunity for attractive color combinations. It can be applied along an edge or included in a seam.

If the material to be used for the piping is firm, like taffeta, etc., cut bias strips an inch and a quarter wide. If a loosely woven material is used, the strips should be a trifle wider. Join all the strips, as described on page 62, and press the seams open. Then fold the strip lengthwise through the center and baste it flat, being careful not to let it become twisted. (Illustration 266.)

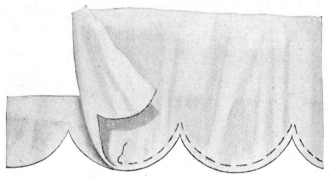

263—The edge basted to tissue-paper

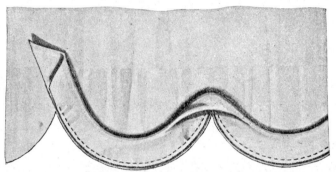

264—The binding stitched to the edge

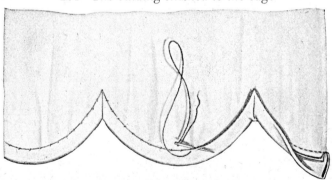

265—The binding rolled to the inside

Binding a Scalloped Edge in Sheer Material

Next prepare the edge of the material to which the piping is to be
applied.   If desired, cut a lining three-eighths of an inch narrower
than the pattern or the piece to be lined.   Baste this lining into
position as shown in Illustration 267.   If the edge forms a fancy

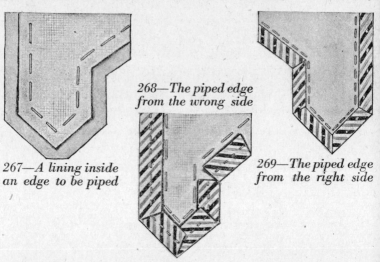

268—The piped edge
from the wrong side

267—A lining inside
an edge to be piped

269—The piped edge
from the right side

outline, as illustrated here, turn the edges over evenly all around,
clipping at the corners and folding in at the points where necessary.
Then run a basting-thread an even width (about three-eighths of an
inch, more or less according to the finished width desired) around
the edge to serve as a guide.   Next baste on the piping, following this line closely.   Be careful to avoid any scantiness at the
points or bulginess at the corners.   (Illustration 268.)   Illustration
269 shows the right side of a pointed edge neatly piped.

Cording

Cording is a very useful trimming.   It is made with bias strips
and Germantown or eider-down wool.   The bias strips should be
about an inch and a quarter wide.   Fold the strips lengthwise
through the center and run a seam a quarter of an inch from the
fold edge.   With the strips still wrong side out slip the ends of
several strands of Germantown or eider-down wool far enough
into one end of the tube-like covering so that you can sew them
securely to it.   Then with the loop end of a wire hairpin push the
wool farther and farther into the covering, at the same time turning
the covering right side out.   (Illustration 270.)

270—Inserting wool into a covering to make a cord

Cord motifs—When cording is used to form a motif, stamp the motif on ordinary wrapping-paper. Baste the cordings in place on the design with the seam uppermost so that the right side of the motif will be next the paper. Then sew them together at the points of intersection and contact. (Illustration 271.)

271—A cord motif

Corded tucks are shown in Illustration 272. The illustration shows the cord being put into the tuck for trimming. Mark the line for the cord with colored thread. Hold the cord underneath with the left hand and enclose it in a tuck, sewing it with fine, even running stitches as close to the cord as possible.

272—Corded tucks

Cord piping is shown in Illustration 273. A bias strip of material is used for the piping. The cord is run in the same way as for tuck cording and the piping is applied to the edge the same way as a plain piping. Or it can be included in a seam.

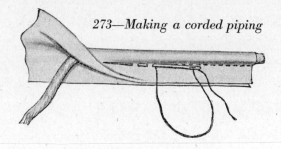

273—*Making a corded piping*

Tie with Ball Trimming

This makes a pretty finish often used at the neck and sleeves of a dress or blouse. (Illustration 279.)

For the ball trimming cut a circle of material 2½ inches (more or less) in diameter. Turn under the edge ¼ inch and gather close to the turning. (Illustration 274.) Roll a piece of sheet wadding into a ball and insert it into the circle. Draw up the thread and fasten. (Illustration 275.)

For the tie cut a strip of material the length desired and twice as wide as the finished tie, with ⅜ inch allowed on all edges for seams. If your material will permit, cut this bias, as it will fall more softly than if straight. Fold the strip in half and stitch it ⅜ inch from the edges. (Illustration 276.) Tack the loop end of a hairpin to one end and push it into the strip, turning it right side out with the seam in one edge. (Illustration 277.) Turn in the ends and slip-stitch them. Gather close to the edge. Draw up the threads and fasten.

Tack the ball to the ends of the tie, leaving ⅛ inch of thread between; buttonhole over the thread. (Illustration 278.)

Bands, Folds and Straps

Bands or folds used as trimming are made in a variety of ways. They may be lined, unlined, double of the material, or piped at the edges. Cut the band the required width, allowing for a turning at each edge.

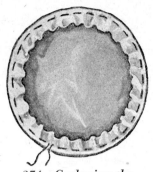

274—Gathering the
circle for the ball

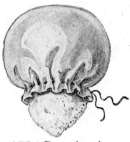

275—Drawing it up
around the wadding

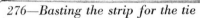

276—Basting the strip for the tie

277—Turning the tie right side out

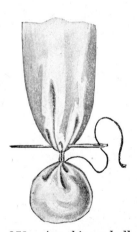

278—Attaching a ball
to an end of the tie

279—The finished tie

A Tie With Ball Trimming

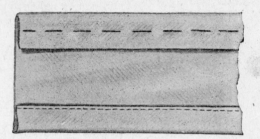

280—An unlined fold is finished at the bottom but the top is basted to the garment before it is stitched

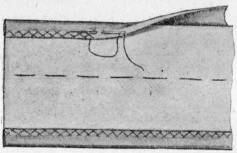

281—In a lined fold the edges are turned over and catch-stitched

282—Piped folds may be edged with plain or corded piping

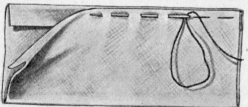

283—Double folds are frequently used instead of tucks

The unlined fold (Illustration 280) is made with its lower edge basted up in a hem and stitched evenly from the right side. The upper edge is turned over, and the band is then basted into position on the garment. The upper edge is stitched through the garment, making the one stitching serve two purposes.

The lined fold is finished before it is applied to the garment. Cut a strip of lining as wide as the band should be when completed. Baste it evenly on the wrong side of the strip of material, turning both edges down over it. Catch-stitch the edges to the lining (Illustration 281) and the fold is ready for use.

The piped fold is one in which a cord or piping (see pages 162 and 166) has been applied to the edges with one or more rows of machine-stitching to give it a tailored finish. (Illustration 282.)

Double folds are made of bias strips cut twice the width desired for the finished band with turnings or seam allowances extra. Fold them over on the center line and baste them flat. Turn the two raw edges in and baste them together. (Illustration 283.) Then join them neatly with slip-stitches and apply to the garment by hand. If machine-stitching is desired, baste the fold in place first and then stitch. These folds are frequently used as a trimming in the place of tucks.

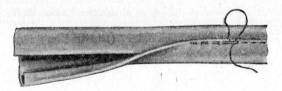

284—Making a milliners' fold

A milliners' fold is made by turning the top edge of the strip over one-half the width of the finished fold and bringing up the lower turned-under edge, to cover the raw upper edge. (Illustration 284.) Sew flat with slip-stitching or fine running stitches. If the material is very sheer, it is a good plan to have a small strip of paper, not quite the width of the fold, to slip along within the fold as the work progresses. If pressing is necessary, use only a warm iron.

Crêpe folds are cut on the straight of the goods, so that the crinkles will run diagonally; in other materials the strip should be bias.

Tailors' straps are folded bands used to strap seams, or as an ornamental trimming on tailored garments. They may be cut on the bias if of velvet or taffeta; crosswise if of woolen; lengthwise if of cotton materials. Fold the strip at the center and catch the raw edges together with loose whip-stitches as shown in Illustration 285. Spread out the fold and press it well. Baste into position on the garment and stitch by machine on both edges.

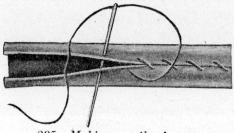

285—Making a tailors' strap

Tie for a Sailor or Middy Blouse

The neckerchief or tie worn with a sailor or middy blouse is a square of black silk tied in a square knot, leaving ends from four to six inches long. It is folded diagonally and then rolled up, with the two overlapping corners folded into the material and held together by an elastic, as shown in Illustration 286, while the other corners are tied at the lower end of the collar in a square knot with a corner extending from each side. (Illustration 287.)

286—A tie for a sailor or middy blouse

287—A square knot with the corners extending from the sides

Chapter XIX

TRIMMING STITCHES

Machine-Hemstitching — French Hemstitching — Picot Edging — Imitation Hand-Hemstitching—Hand-Hemstitching—Rolled Edges—Fagoting and Beading—Bar Tack—Crow's-Foot Tack—Arrowhead Tack—Feather-Stitching—Smocking—Pompon—Fringe—Twisted Cord—Tassel

MACHINE-HEMSTITCHING is used on blouses, dresses, lingerie, etc., to put together seams, finish hems and put on trimmings such as bands, etc. It is neat, durable and gives a garment a dainty, finished look.

It is also used as a trimming either in straight rows or in a fancy design. Prices for the work vary, but it is not expensive and any plaiting establishment or the salesroom of a sewing-machine company will do it.

The line or seam for machine-hemstitching should always be basted in self-colored thread so that the basting need not be removed. (Illustration 288.) Removing the basting cuts the hemstitching. Only one mark is necessary for French hemstitching.

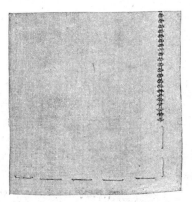

288—The line for machine-hemstitching should always be basted in self-colored thread

Seams on which machine-hemstitching is used as a trimming or finish should be basted flat with both edges of the seam turned toward the left side (Illustration 289) and pressed. An invisible seam for transparent materials can be made by machine-hemstitching an ordinary seam. (Illustration 290.) The seam is basted in the usual way and the hemstitching is done on the wrong side of the garment just outside the basting. The seam edges are then trimmed off.

In machine-hemstitching keep the garment as nearly flat as possible. Seams that are not to be hemstitched should not be basted or sewed until after the hemstitching is done, for if they are left open it will be possible to keep the garment much flatter. If a cuff is to be hemstitched to a sleeve, leave the sleeve seam open until the hemstitching is done.

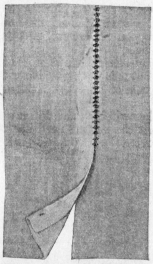 

289—A seam finished with machine-hemstitching

290—An invisible seam for transparent materials

A foundation for machine-hemstitching is necessary under bias edges such as shaped collars (Illustration 291), under thin materials (Illustration 292) and for French hemstitching (Illustration 293) (several rows of hemstitching placed close together).

The foundation for such materials as net, Georgette crêpe, chiffon, lace, etc., may be mousseline-de-soie or very thin lawn.

The foundation for machine-hemstitching done on the bias of the material can be a straight strip of the same material or of the foundations mentioned above, about one-half inch wide basted underneath the line to be hemstitched. (Illustration 294.) If no material for a foundation is at hand, baste the article to a piece of firm paper and stitch it by machine along the line for the hemstitching. (Illustration 295.) This stitching keeps the edge from stretching and gives the operator the correct line for machine-hemstitching. The paper should be torn away before the material is sent to the operator. Paper can also be used in this way under straight edges of thin material when you do not wish to use a foundation.

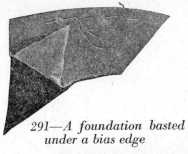

291—*A foundation basted under a bias edge*

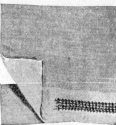

293—*French hemstitching*

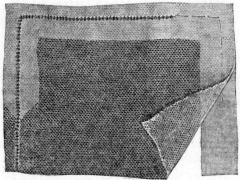

292—*A foundation under a thin material*

294—*A foundation under a line on the bias of the material*

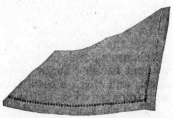

295—*Machine-stitching marking the line for hemstitching*

French hemstitching is the term used to describe several rows of hemstitching placed close together. This requires a foundation when it is done on either thick or thin material. (Illustration 293.) The foundation can be of the same material or of the foundations mentioned above. The seams or foundations are cut away close to the hemstitching after the hemstitching is done. On edges other than seam edges when there is a single thickness of material leave about three-eighths of an inch of material outside the line of hemstitching.

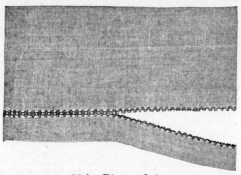

296—Picot edging

Picot edging is simply machine-hemstitching cut through the center. (Illustration 296.) It makes a very dainty and yet strong finish for edges of collars, sleeves, tunics, ruffles, sashes, etc.

Imitation hand-hemstitching—This is done on the machine and can be worked in two ways. The first way is described on page 80. Illustrations 297 and 298 show a form that is often used on house linens and sometimes on garments to join seams or attach an applied hem or facing. It can be used only when two edges are to be joined.

Fold blotting-paper or other soft paper until you have a thickness of about ⅛ inch. Lay the two edges of the material together as for a plain seam and insert the blotting-paper between them. Loosen the tension of the machine, adjust it for a medium-length stitch, use a needle coarse enough to go through the blotting-paper without bending and a thread heavy enough to give the desired effect, and stitch a seam through all thicknesses a quarter of an inch from the edge. (Illustration 297.)

When the seam is stitched, cut the paper close to the stitching and pull it away. The stitches between the two pieces of material will then look like Illustration 298.

Turn each edge away from the hemstitching and stitch or baste flat. When a hem is being applied, turn it up over the raw edge and stitch close to the hemstitching or hem by hand. Stitch the other edge flat and cut off close to the stitching or finish with a tiny hem or rolled edge. When using this stitching to put seam edges together, turn both edges away from the hemstitching and stitch close to the fold or finish with a tiny hem or rolled edge as desired.

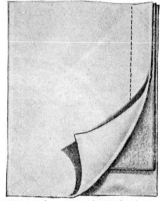
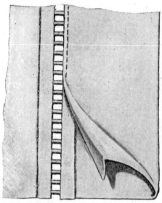

297—A seam stitched for imitation hand-hemstitching

298—The effect with paper removed and edges turned back

Hand-Hemstitching

Hand-hemstitching is a line of openwork made by drawing out parallel threads and fastening the cross threads in successive small clusters. Draw as many threads of the material as desired at the top of the hem, and baste it on this line. Hold the hem toward you and work on the side on which it is turned up.

Plain hemstitching—Hemstitching may be done from left to right or from right to left, but many people find the first way the easier. Insert the needle in the under fold of the hem at the left-hand edge. Hold the work over the forefinger of the left hand, keeping the thumb over the thread. Take up four or five threads with the needle, and draw the needle through, holding the sewing thread firmly by the left thumb. At the extreme right of the gathered threads take a short stitch in the fold of the hem, as shown in

Illustration 299, and draw the thread through. Now take up the same number of threads as before, and repeat. Care must be taken to keep the warp and woof threads exactly parallel, especially in hemstitching a corner where the material has not been cut away.

Double hemstitching—Draw the threads as for plain hemstitching and baste the hem in the same way. Work the first line as described for plain hemstitching or insert the needle in the under fold of the extreme right and work from right to left, holding the work over the forefinger of the left hand. Hold the thread under the thumb and take up four or five threads with the needle, bringing the needle out over the thread so that it forms a loop as shown in Illustration 300. Draw this loop quite tight and take a small stitch to the left of the stitch in the fold of the hem. Now take up the same number of threads as before and repeat the hemstitching for the length of your hem. When it is finished, turn your work so that the opposite side of the drawn threads is toward you. Make a second row of hemstitching in the same way, taking up the same groups of thread as before. (Illustration 300.) Take the little stitch between the groups through the edges of the material instead of through the fold of the hem as in the first row.

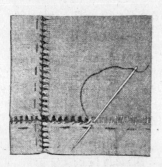

299—Plain hemstitching

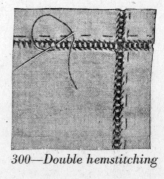

300—Double hemstitching

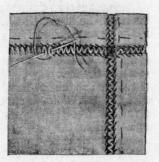

301—Serpentine or fagot hemstitching

Serpentine or fagot hemstitching is worked the same as double hemstitching except that in the second row of stitches half of the threads of one cluster and half of the threads of the next cluster are grouped together, giving a slanting or serpentine effect. (Illustration 301.) For this type of hemstitching the groups must contain an even number of drawn threads so that they can be divided evenly. Otherwise the effect of the clusters will be irregular and uneven when finished.

Fagoting and Beading

The fagot-stitch is a style of hand-made trimming that is always popular and attractive. (Illustration 302.)

For fagoting, the design of the work should first be traced on a piece of stiff paper. Or, as in the case of a yoke or collar where a fitted shaping is required, a fitted pattern should be cut of stiff paper, and the ribbon, braid or folds of the material basted evenly in position, following all the curves. When the fagoting is to be applied to the garment in fancy design, and the material underneath the stitches is to be cut away afterward, the entire piece of work should be smoothly basted over paper, and the line of spacing which represents the fagot-stitching outlined with chalk or basting cotton.

The simple fagot-stitch is done by crossing first from left to right and recrossing from side to side between the folds of the material, taking a small stitch in the edge. The needle in crossing each time passes under the thread of the preceding stitch, thus giving the threads a slight twist at the edge of the material. (Illustration 302.)

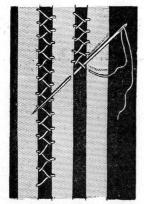

302—The simple fagot-stitch, easily worked but effective

303—Two of the simpler varieties of beading stitches

Simple beading stitches are shown in Illustration 303.

To make the design on the right, a buttonholed bar, take a stitch directly across the space between the two folds and work the buttonhole-stitch over the thread back to the starting-point. Then stick the needle into the edge of the fold near the hole of the first stitch to keep the bar from twisting, and on the under side pass on to position for the next bar.

In the left-hand design, a link bar, carry the thread across as in the other case and take a small stitch along the edge. Returning, make one loose buttonhole-stitch over the thread. Over this same loop run two closer buttonhole-stitches. Then make a second loose buttonhole-stitch over the first thread, and again, as before, the two close buttonhole-stitches over this loop. Catch the needle into the edge of the fold, and pass on to the next stitch. The link bar is not so difficult to make as it appears, and really can be done more quickly than the plain buttonhole-bar.

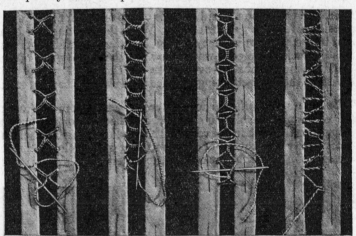

304—More elaborate stitches which may be used merely as trimmings or as beadings through which to run ribbons

More elaborate beading stitches are shown in Illustration 304. The right-hand design is a combination of the link bar (described in the preceding paragraph) run diagonally across the open space, and a simple twisted stitch run straight across from the apex of each of the triangles thus made.

To make the second design from the right in Illustration 304, bring the thread up from one edge of the fold over to the opposite edge, take a stitch from the under side and draw the thread taut.

Then insert the needle three-eighths of an inch from that point,
allowing the thread to form a tiny loop. Insert the needle again
directly opposite the last hole, and from this point make five buttonhole-stitches in the loop. Now catch up the edge of the fold
just where the first plain stitch began, and on the under side
bring it over to the second plain stitch, and draw it up for the
next loop.

In the third design from the right in Illustration 304, carry the
thread across from one fold to the other and leave it rather loose.
Then bring the thread up through the same fold one-quarter of an
inch from the point where it was just inserted. Make five buttonhole-stitches in the loop formed of the thread in crossing, and insert
the needle in the opposite edge.
Now carry the thread over again to form the next loop, running
the needle into the same hole. Bring it up one-quarter of an inch
below this point, and continue as before.

To make the buttonhole cross-bar stitch illustrated in the fourth
design of Illustration 304, first make a buttonholed bar as described
in the paragraph on simple beading stitches but do not draw it
tight; rather let it curve a trifle. Then proceed as if for the next
bar, but when crossing catch into the preceding bar at the center
buttonhole-stitch, and then continue to the opposite edge. Make
an even number of buttonhole-stitches on each side on this thread.
Allow a small space between the cross-bars.

Rolled Edges

Rolled edges are used as a trimming on blouses and dresses of
thin materials and also on children's clothes. They are worked
with twisted embroidery silk on silk materials and with mercerized
cotton on cotton materials. Either self or contrasting colors may
be used. Hold the right side of the material toward you. Begin at the right end and roll the edge toward you between the
thumb and forefinger of the left hand, keeping the edge rolled for
about one and a half inch ahead of the sewing. Fasten the thread

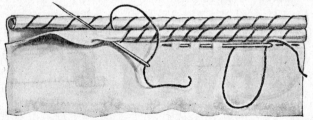

305—Rolled edges used as trimming

at the right and take slanting stitches over the roll. The stitches should be about one-quarter of an inch apart. Do not draw the thread tight. (Illustration 305.)

Where two edges are joined, as in a blouse with a fancy lining, both edges should be rolled separately. Place the rolled edge of the outer part directly beneath the rolled edge of the under part. (Illustration 305.) Sew them together with running stitches about one-quarter of an inch long just below the lower roll.

Tacks

For working these ornamental tacks, coarse buttonhole twist or twisted embroidery silk is usually employed, and it is generally the same color as the material. With a little practise these tacks can be well made, and any of them will add greatly to the finish of the garment.

Bar tacks make a very neat and serviceable finish for the ends of seams, tucks and plaits, and the corners of collars, pockets and pocket-laps of tailored garments. Illustration 306 shows the process of making the simple bar tack, generally used as a stay for pocket openings.

Mark the length desired for the tack, stick the needle through the entire thickness of the goods, down on one side, up on the opposite, and repeat several times, according to the required strength of the tack. Then without breaking off the thread, make one short stitch across one end of the long ones, and continue stitching closely all the way across, firmly covering the threads of the long stitches.

Keep these cross-stitches close together, and while working press the long stitches with the needle, in order to produce a cord-like effect.

On garments having a finish of machine-stitches at pocket openings, etc., the bar tack, with small bars crossing the ends of the plain bar, is more ornamental. (Illustration 307.) The process of making is similar to that of the simple bar tack, with small bars worked in after the long one has been finished.

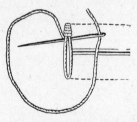

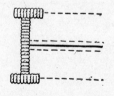

306—The method of work-
ing a plain bar tack

307—A bar tack with
small bars at the end

The crow's-foot tack is the most ornamental of the fancy tacks ordinarily used at the ends of pocket openings and seams. It is shown in Illustration 310, with the details of the stitch in Illustrations 308 and 309.

The crow's-foot is generally worked in scarlet or dark blue silk on the pockets of serge sailor suits. When it is used to finish the end of a plait in a skirt, it is worked in floss the color of the dress.

Outline the tack with chalk or pencil. The dotted outline seen in Illustration 308 shows the correct design for the tack. Bring the needle up at point A, pass it down at B, and up again at B outside of and close to the stitch in line AB; then down at C, up at C outside of and close to the stitch in line BC, and down at A just outside the stitch in line AB, as illustrated in Illustration 308. Now bring the needle up on the dotted line AC outside the stitch on line AC close to A; pass it down on dotted line BC outside the stitch on line BC close to B; up on dotted line AB outside both stitches on line AB close to B; down on dotted line CA outside the stitch on line CA close to C; up on dotted line BC outside both stitches on line BC; and down on dotted line AB outside both stitches on line AB, as shown in Illustration 309. Fill in the entire outline in this way until the completed tack looks like Illustration 310. It will be noticed in making this tack that all the stitches are taken on the dotted lines and always outside the made stitches, thus compressing the first stitches so as to curve the sides of the tack like the outline.

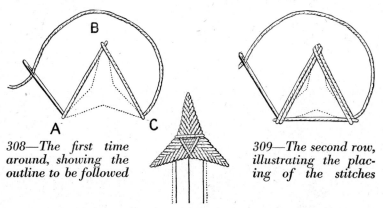

308—The first time around, showing the outline to be followed

309—The second row, illustrating the placing of the stitches

310—The crow's-foot tack, the most ornamental of the tacks ordinarily used at the ends of plaits, laps, seams and pocket openings

Arrow-head tacks are used at the top or bottom of plaits and laps and at the ends of seams and pocket openings.

First make an outline of the arrow with chalk or pencil. Illustrations 311 and 312 show the triangular shape of the outline. Bring the needle up at point A, then take a small stitch at point B as shown by the position of the needle in Illustration 311. Bring the needle down at point C (Illustration 312), up very close to point A along the line CA (Illustration 312), and take another stitch at

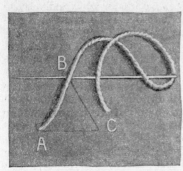

311—*The first stitch*

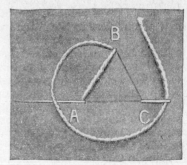

312—*The second stitch*

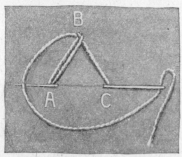

313—*Filling in the outline*

314—*The arrow-head tack for the ends of plaits, laps, seams and pocket openings*

point B close under the first one, then down very close to point C along the line CA. (Illustration 313.) The needle must go in on the chalk line BC and come up on the chalk line BA, keeping the outline of the triangle. Each successive parallel stitch below point B will be a little longer than the previous one. Repeat this stitch until the entire space is filled. The completed arrow-head is shown in Illustration 314. It makes a neat, attractive finish.

Feather-Stitching

The feather-stitch is one of the most frequently used of all ornamental stitches, for it can be worked with the coarsest of yarn or
the finest of silk, linen, or cotton thread according to the nature
of the material on which it is used.   It makes a most satisfactory
trimming.   The single, double and triple combinations are shown
in Illustration 315.

Run a colored thread along the outline to mark the center line
for the feather-stitching.   To make the single stitch, knot the
thread and then bring the needle up through the material.   Hold
the thread down over the line with the left thumb.   Insert the
needle a little to the left of this line, and take a short, slanting
stitch toward the right, drawing the needle out while the thread is
held down smoothly by the left thumb.   Then hold down the
thread on the center line and take a stitch of equal length on the
right side and draw it out as before.

For the double combination take two stitches to the left and two
to the right each time before crossing the center line, and for the
triple combination take three stitches.   The beauty of feather-
stitching depends on its evenness.   Marks on the illustration indicate the position and direction for the stitches.

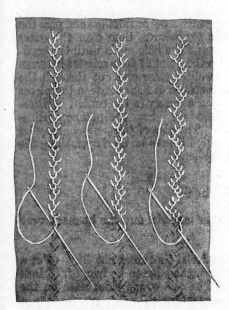

*315—Single, double and
triple feather-stitching.
The marks below the
stitching indicate the
position of the stitches
to be made*

Smocking

Smocking is a style of trimming particularly suited to children's clothes, and much used on the better class of children's garments here and abroad. It is used for dresses, rompers, coats and little boys' suits. It is very pretty in colors on dresses of fine white batiste, nainsook, plain lawn, handkerchief linen, cotton voile, very fine cotton crêpe and silk mull. It is also used on the heavier cotton materials in white or plain colors, on chambray, serge, broadcloth, crêpe de Chine, etc. As a trimming it is sufficiently ornamental to make the addition of other decoration quite unnecessary; and as an inexpensive trimming it can not be equaled. It is very easy to do with the Butterick transfers, which not only give the design of the smocking but instructions for working it.

In a Butterick design that shows smocking, the transfer is sometimes included in the pattern. If not, a transfer number is given that is suitable for the garment. It is the best plan to use only this transfer because it will take up just the amount of fulness allowed in the pattern. Any other transfer would not work out so successfully.

Pompon

Cut two circles of cardboard 3¼ inches (more or less) in diameter. Lay the two circles together and punch a hole through the center. Thread a darning-needle with wool or silk floss and pass the needle through the hole in the cardboards, then over the outer edge of the cardboards and through the hole again until the cardboards are thickly covered. Slip the point of your scissors between the pieces of cardboard at the outer edge and cut through the floss. (Illustration 316.) Slip a strand of floss between the pieces of cardboard and tie the pompon securely in the center. (Illustration 317.) Slip the cardboards off. Sew the pompon (Illustration 318) to hat or costume. The size of the pompon may be varied to suit the purpose for which it is to be used by making the circles of cardboard larger or smaller.

Fringe

Fringe is sometimes made of the material and can be made very easily and quickly.

Cut fringe can be made on material that does not fray. Put a basting the required distance from the edge to be fringed. Mark spaces with chalk ¼ inch apart on the wrong side; slash on the chalk lines to the basting. (Illustration 319.)

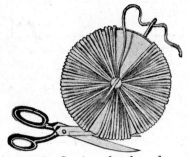

316—Cutting the thread
around the edge

317—Tying the thread
in the center

318—A finished pompon
suitable for hat or costume

319—Cut fringe

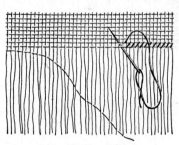

320—Drawn fringe

Drawn fringe may be made on a straight edge of any material the threads of which pull easily and are heavy enough to form a pretty fringe. Pull out crosswise threads of material to the depth the fringe is to be, pulling one thread at a time. After the threads have been drawn, overcast the last thread to the thread above to prevent raveling. (Illustration 320.)

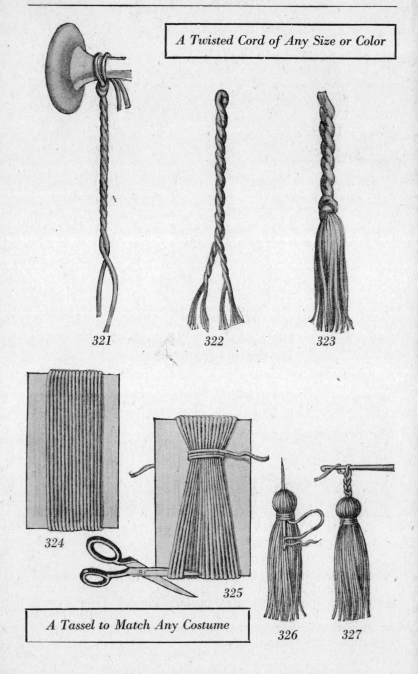

A Twisted Cord of Any Size or Color

321

322

323

324

325

A Tassel to Match Any Costume

326   327

Twisted Cord

A twisted cord may be made in any size, from one of embroidery floss or fine cord for the neck of a blouse or dress to a heavy cord for a bathrobe. The method of making is the same, but keep in mind that the cord when finished will be about four times as thick as the thread or cord you started with and less than one-half as long, because the twisting shortens the length—just how much depends on the size of the thread or cord.

Cut two strands of floss or cord each a little more than twice the desired length. Tie the strands to a knob. Twist tightly toward the right. (Illustration 321.) Unfasten from the knob, holding the ends together, and fold in half. Twist toward right—release the folded end, forming a twisted cord. (Illustration 322.)

Make a knot the desired distance from the loose ends, and fray out the ends, forming a tassel below the knot. (Illustration 323.) The other end may be finished to match, if desired.

Tassel

It is not always possible to purchase a tassel of just the right size and color desired and it is very easy to make one.

Cut a cardboard a little longer than the tassel is to be and one-half as wide.

Cover it with embroidery thread, rope silk, wool or fine cord, depending on the purpose for which the tassel is to be used. (Illustration 324.)

Draw the strands together on each side of the cardboard ¾ of an inch more or less from the top, and tack. Cut through threads at the bottom. (Illustration 325.)

Fasten at the tacks and wind the thread around several times. Pass the needle to the top. (Illustration 326.)

Pass two threads over the top of the tassel. Buttonhole across, covering these threads.

With the same thread make chain-stitches about ¾ inch long. (Illustration 327.) Tack the tassel to position.

Chapter XX

RUFFLES, EMBROIDERY AND LACE

Ruffles—Embroidery Used as a Facing—Embroidery Joined in a Tuck—
Embroidery Inserted with Rolled Hems—Embroidery Inserted by Machine—
Embroidery Mitered—Whipping on Trimming—Inserting Lace—Inserting
Lace Above a Facing—Mitering Lace—Shaped Pieces of Insertion—Inserting
Lace Medallions

A RUFFLE used as trimming may be attached in various ways.
For a whipped and gathered ruffle, roll the raw edge and
overcast the material as far as it is rolled, taking care to
make the stitch below the roll, not through it. (Illustration 328.)
Draw up the thread, making the ruffle the desired fulness. Divide
the ruffle in quarters and mark them with colored thread. Make
corresponding marks on the edge to which the ruffle is to be
attached. Roll the edge of the garment and overhand the ruffle
to it, taking a stitch in every whipped stitch of the ruffle.

To insert a ruffle in a hem turn the hem toward the right side of
the garment and crease the fold hard. Divide both ruffle and hem
in quarters and mark each division with colored thread. Insert
the edge of the ruffle in the hem close to the fold (Illustration 329)
with the right side of the ruffle to the right side of the garment and
the corresponding marks together. Baste and stitch one-quarter
of an inch from the fold. Turn the hem back to the wrong side
of the garment, fold the second turning, baste and hem. (Illustration 330.)

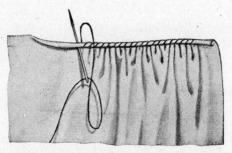

328—A whipped and gathered ruffle

188

329—Inserting a ruffle in a hem

330—The hem turned and stitched

331—Covering the joining of a ruffle

To cover the joining of a ruffle, divide both ruffle and garment in quarters and mark with pins or colored thread. Gather the ruffle and baste it to the garment. Turn the raw edges up on the garment and cover with a narrow bias band which can be bought by the piece with the edges turned ready for use. (Illustration 331.) This finish may be used on either the right or wrong side of the garment. Frequently this finish is used on scalloped or plain edges that are not lined or faced.

Embroidery Edging and Insertion

Embroidery edging used as a facing is shown in Illustration 332. The plain material above the embroidery is applied as the facing. Crease the edging off at the depth it is to extend beyond the garment. Baste the material along the crease so that the seam will come toward the inside of the garment. Then stitch the seam. Now turn the edging down, fold in the raw edge at the top, and hem down as a facing. The facing should be no wider than necessary to make a neat joining.

To join embroidery in a tuck, make several tucks in the plain material above the embroidery if it is wide enough. Then measure carefully the amount for the space between the tucks, the under part of the tucks and the seam. Cut away the superfluous material and join the edging to the garment. Crease the tuck with the seam directly in the folds so that the raw edges will be encased in the tuck. When the materials of the garment and the embroidery are similar, and there are several tucks above and below the seam, the joining is imperceptible. (Illustration 333.)

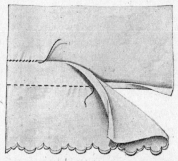 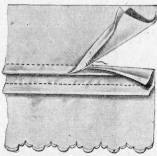

332—*Embroidery edging used as a facing*   333—*Embroidery edging joined in a tuck*

Embroidery may be inserted by different methods. When a straight-edge insertion is used, the plain material may be cut away at each side of the embroidery, and the material of the garment cut away under the embroidery, leaving a small seam, which is rolled and whipped to the embroidery as shown in Illustration 334.

Seam binding may be inserted by the same method used in Illustration 334.

A rolled hem may be used as a dainty finish in joining trimming of any kind to a garment of sheer wash material. Hold the wrong side of the material toward you, and, after trimming off all ravel-

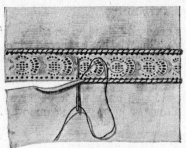
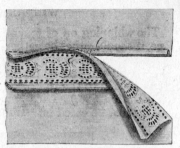

*334—Inserting embroidery with   335—Inserting embroidery
a rolled edge   with a French seam*

ings, begin at the right end and roll the edge toward you tightly
between the thumb and forefinger of the left hand, keeping the edge
rolled for about one and a half inch ahead of the sewing. (Illustration 334.)

If preferred, a small seam may be left on the insertion as well
as on the garment and they may be put together by a tiny French
seam. (Illustration 335.) This is the finish most commonly employed.

Embroidery also may be inserted by a machine fell seam. Baste
the insertion to the material with a narrow seam on the wrong side;
trim off all ravelings; insert the raw edges in the hemmer of the
machine, and stitch as in hemming.

Embroidery trimming may be mitered so that the joining will
scarcely be seen. Fold it over so that the crease comes exactly in
the middle of the corner, taking care to match the pattern perfectly. Crease firmly and cut on the creased line. (Illustration 336.)
Place the right sides face to face and buttonhole the raw edges
together with short, close stitches. Illustration 337 shows the
finished corner. The method of making the buttonhole-stitch is
shown in Illustration 221 on page 143.

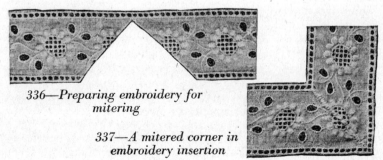

*336—Preparing embroidery for
mitering*

*337—A mitered corner in
embroidery insertion*

Whipping on Trimming

The whipping on of trimming is generally done on an edge. If lace, it should either be gathered by pulling the heavy thread which is usually found at the top, or whipped and drawn as in a ruffle. Roll an inch or two of the garment material, place the lace with its right side to the right side of the material, and whip together. (Illustration 338.) Lace may be whipped on plain if preferred, but it must be eased in. Insertion may be inset in the same way.

338—Whipping on a lace edging

Lace

Methods of applying lace edging and insertion, when the material has a straight edge, are shown in Illustrations 339-342.

To edge a hem with lace and insert lace between hems, fold the material for a hem, creasing the lower fold hard. Open the hem and baste the lace edge just below the lower fold, and stitch. (Illustration 339.) Turn back the hem and crease the material on a line with the top turning of the hem. (Illustration 339.) Cut to within a small seam above this crease. Fold in the raw edge, insert the edge of the lace insertion (Illustration 340), and stitch. Turn a second hem, following these directions, baste the other edge of the insertion just below the lower crease, and stitch as before. As many rows of insertion may be used in this manner as are desired.

Insertion above a facing is first basted in position and the upper edge is finished as shown in Illustration 341. The facing is generally used when the outline of the edge is curved or pointed so that it can not be turned up in a straight hem.

Draw the pull-thread in the lace where a curve requires a slight gathering to make it lie flat. The facing is cut to fit the outline of the outer edge and applied as a false hem, as shown in Illustration

341.   When edging is used, it is basted to the bottom before the facing is added and all are stitched in a seam together.   Turn under the facing at the line of sewing, baste in position and stitch the insertion from the right side.

To insert lace insertion in a garment, pin the lace in the position desired and baste down both edges of the insertion.

If the insertion is narrow, cut the material through the center (Illustration 342); but if the insertion is wide, cut the material away from underneath, simply allowing a seam on each side.   Turn the edge in a narrow hem covering the line of the basting.   Stitch the insertion close to the edges from the right side, at the same time catching through the material of the hem.

9—Lace applied on the edge of a hem

40—Lace inserted between hems

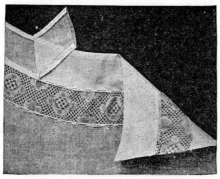

41—Lace inserted above a facing on a curved edge

342—Applying narrow lace insertion

To miter lace—The lace should be cut between the cords, not across them. Overhand the edges together, putting the needle back the depth of two cords. Illustration 343 shows the figures cut around the edge, lapped and hemmed around the figure on each side. For a stronger corner, the lace may be mitered in a very tiny, flat hem. (Illustration 344.)

343—*Lace mitered with
an overhanded seam*

344—*Lace mitered with
a tiny flat hem*

Joining rows of lace to fit a curve—A shaped piece made of rows of insertion joined together is made over a piece of stiff paper. Cut a piece of stiff paper the size and shape of what you are making and baste the rows of insertion to the paper so that the edges of the rows just meet. (Illustration 345.) Begin with the longest row of insertion and baste the longest edge of that row to the paper with the right side down. Draw the pull-thread at the other edge of the same row to draw it into a curve. If you are careful in distributing the fulness evenly, most of it can be pressed out, unless the curve is very great. Whip the edges of the rows together and press them before removing them from the paper. (Illustration 345.)

345—*Rows of lace joined to fit a curve*

To insert lace medallions, baste them to the material and stitch them by machine as close to the edge as possible.

Cut out the material from under the lace, leaving a narrow seam's width all around. (Illustration 346.) This edge may be turned back and stitched flat by a second row of stitching, leaving a raw edge. Or, it may be overcast closely with the raw edge rolled in to prevent any possible raveling. Illustration 346 shows a medallion set in this way.

Sometimes, where two finished edges come together, they are lapped and stitched together as shown in Illustration 347.

346—A lace medallion inset with raw edges rolled and overcast

347—A medallion inset with straight edges lapped and stitched

Chapter XXI

SHIRRINGS, PUFFINGS, RUCHES AND PLAITINGS

Gathering—Shirring—Scalloped or Snail Shirrings—Cord Shirrings—Simple Ruche—Three-Tuck Ruche—Box-Plaited or Gathered Ruches—Ruche of Frayed Taffeta—Double Ruche with One Cord Shirring—Double Ruche with Two Cord Shirrings

FOR the shirred trimmings given in this chapter the softest materials should be used.

Plaited trimmings may be made of very soft materials or of materials with more body.

Soft ribbons requiring no finish at the edges may be used effectively for these trimmings.

Most materials for the ruchings and puffings may be cut bias or straight.

Chiffon should always be cut lengthwise or crosswise, never bias.

Silks and satins lie in softer folds if they are cut bias or crosswise.

If the edges are to be frayed, the materials must be cut lengthwise or crosswise. Crosswise is preferable, for the warp threads are usually closer and make a thicker fringe.

If net is to be used with raw edges, it should be cut on the line of the straight threads which run lengthwise, or bias. You can easily determine the direction of these threads on the piece you are using by stretching the net a little in different directions. Net is more easily hemmed if cut as above, but for a double ruche it may be cut lengthwise, crosswise or bias.

Different materials require different amounts of fulness for shirred ruches. A soft fabric such as chiffon requires three times the length of the finished ruche. Taffeta and such materials which have a little more body require only about twice the finished length.

Gathering

For gathering make a row of small running stitches. The stitches may be the same length as the spaces, or the spaces may be twice the length of the stitches. Always begin by inserting the needle from the wrong side to conceal the knot. It is better to slip the stitches along on the needle and not remove it from the material.

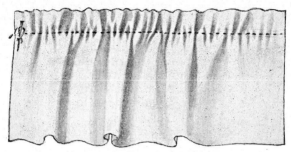

348—Plain gathering

With a single row of gathering it is necessary to stroke the stitches in order to make them lie straight. When the gathering is completed, remove the needle and draw the gatherings up tight. Place a pin vertically, close to the last stitch, and wind the thread several times around the pin in the form of an 8. (Illustration 348.) This holds the gathers firmly together.

Hold the work between the thumb and fingers of the left hand, with the thumb below the gathering-thread. Put the side of the needle well above the gathering-thread and press the little plait

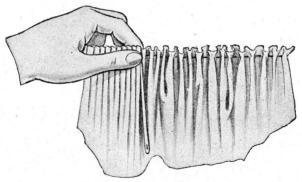

349—Stroking a single row of gathers

under the thumb, drawing the needle down.   (Illustration 349.)
Do not turn the point of the needle toward the material, as it
scratches and weakens the material.   Continue entirely across the
gathers, putting the needle under each stitch and holding the plait
firmly with the thumb.   Stroke the material above the gathering
thread as well as below it to make the gathers firm and even.

Two rows of gathers are often used in dressmaking and do not
need stroking.   A skirt joined to a band, a sleeve set in a cuff or
sewed into the armhole, should be gathered twice so that the
gathers will stay in the proper place.

The second row is made with the stitches directly in line with
those of the first row and one-quarter or three-eighths of an inch
below them.   (Illustration 350.)   If there is much fulness to be
gathered, the spaces between the stitches may be lengthened.

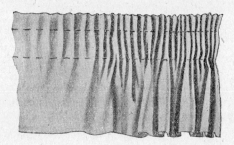

*350—Two rows
of gathers*

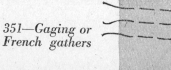

*351—Gaging or
French gathers*

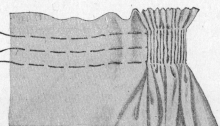

Gaging or French gathers—This is a style of shirring generally used
where a quantity of material must be adjusted to a comparatively
small space.   (Illustration 351.)   The stitches in this case are
made unevenly: long ones on the right side and short ones on the
under side of the material.   Each successive row of gathers has
its long and short stitches parallel, respectively, with those of the
preceding row.   The threads are all drawn up evenly and fastened
at the ends.

Shirring

Shirring is made of successive rows of gatherings.   It is used as a trimming.   There are several different kinds of shirring, the use of which must be determined somewhat by the character of the material and the style of the garment.   Before beginning, it is best to mark the sewing lines with a colored thread to be sure to get the rows even.   This thread can be drawn out when the shirring is finished.

A simple shirring is shown in Illustration 352.   The top edge is turned in and the first row shirred in close to the edge.   The thread should be amply strong, with a good big knot at the end; for if the thread is weak and breaks, or the knot pulls through, the shirring will progress slowly, and the material will suffer unnecessarily in the working.

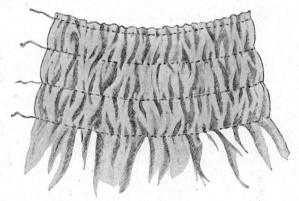

352—A simple shirring

Scallops or snail shirrings are meant to be used as a band trimming.   Make a narrow fold of the material, and run the shirring thread zigzag across from edge to edge.   (Illustration 353.)   As the work progresses, draw up the thread and the fold will acquire a scallop edge on both sides.   If a wider fold is used, two threads may be run in close together.   This will produce a more even trimming and one that will be less perishable.

353—Scallops or snail shirrings

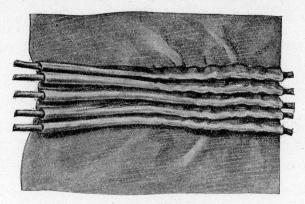

354—Cord shirring

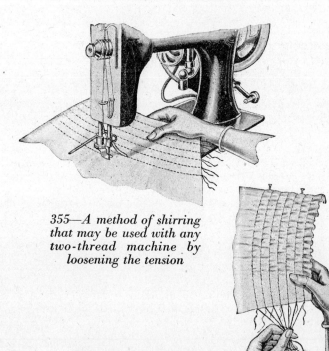

*355—A method of shirring
that may be used with any
two-thread machine by
loosening the tension*

*356—Drawing up the
tighter under threads and
pushing the material along
to form the shirring*

Cord shirring (Illustration 354) is made by sewing tiny tucks with a cord enclosed from the underside. When all the threads have been run in, draw up the fulness.

Shirring by machine—Shirring can also be done very successfully on the machine by using the gathering attachment. In that case it is especially necessary to mark the first sewing line before beginning, as the machine does the work so rapidly that one is more apt to get an irregular line. Successive lines may be put in accurately by using the gage that comes with the machine.

Another method of shirring by any machine that has a double thread is to stitch in the ordinary way with a rather loose tension on the thread.

Use a medium-length stitch. If the pattern has no perforations to guide you; use the gage for spacing stitchings evenly. (Illustration 355.)

Pin the center of the stitchings to a table, or any flat surface. Hold all the under threads together with one hand. With the other hand, push the material back on the threads to form shirrings, being careful not to break the threads. (Illustration 356.)

Ruches

The width of ruches—For single ruches with cords you must allow from one-quarter to one-half inch for each cord, the amount depending on the size of the cord. If the edges are to be hemmed or rolled, sufficient allowance should be made for that finish.

For a double ruche calculate the width of a single ruche and double the amount.

Clean even edges are important, especially if the ruche is to be frayed. The best way to get a good edge for strips cut crosswise or lengthwise is to pull a thread of the material.

The edges of single ruches may be finished in different ways, depending on the material. Taffeta may be frayed, pinked, picoted or finished with tiny hems.

Crêpe de Chine can be frayed, picoted or hemmed.

Chiffon may have its edges picoted, or rolled and whipped tightly with fine stitches in the same or contrasting color.

Net may be picoted, hemmed with same or contrasting color, or, if it is a fine mesh, cut in such a way that the edge needs no finish.

Strips should be joined as neatly as possible. Some nets can be seamed with an over-and-over stitch, using No. 150 cotton. The joining can scarcely be detected. If this is not desirable for the net you are using, make a plain seam and trim the edges down to within one-eighth of an inch of the stitching. Roll the seam edges down to the stitching and whip them closely.

Non-transparent materials may be joined in a plain seam for a double ruche. For a single ruche they should be joined with a tiny French seam. This can be trimmed away under a frayed edge so that the frayed edge appears continuous. This work must be done very carefully.

In cutting, plan the strips so that as few joinings as possible are required.

357—A simple ruche

358—A three-tuck ruche

A simple ruche can be made from strips of the material. Cut off the selvedge, for the selvedge is stiff and would prevent the material from making a soft ruche. Join as many strips of material as are necessary to make the ruche the desired length. Turn under one raw edge of the strip and fold the strip so that it will be double, with the seam at the center of the under side. Gather the ruche through the center just inside the fold edge. (Illustration 357.)

A three-tuck ruche is used when more fulness is desired than is given by a simple ruche. This is made by cutting the strips about seven inches wide. After joining the strips as before, fold them lengthwise in thirds, bringing the two raw edges together three-eighths of an inch from the folds.   Run a gathering-thread through all the layers at one time.   (Illustration 358.)

A ruche of frayed taffeta is shown in Illustration 359.   The silk is cut single and there is one cord shirring.

A double ruche with one cording—The edges of the material are folded over until they just meet at the center of the strip and are basted in place.   The strip is then folded lengthwise through the center and a line of fine running stitches forms a tuck.   (Illustration 360.)   The cord may be inserted while making the tuck. (Illustration 360.)

For two fine cordings the sewing of each tuck should be about one-eighth of an inch from the center.   If larger cords are used, the sewing of the tucks should be a little farther apart so as not to crowd them.

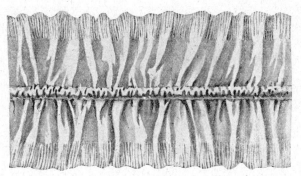

359—*A ruche of frayed taffeta*

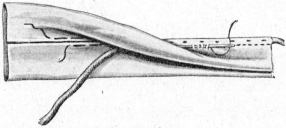

360—*A double ruche with one cording*

Chapter XXII

BRAID, APPLIQUÉ, OSTRICH, MARABOU AND FUR

Flat or Tubular Braid—Soutache Braid—Rickrack Braid—Appliqué Embroidery—Ostrich—Marabou—Fur

BRAIDING makes a very effective trimming and the work goes quickly so that even when deep bandings are in fashion one can have a handsome costume with a comparatively small amount of work and expense. All the newest and smartest transfer designs for braiding will be found in NEEDLE-ART, while DELINEATOR and the QUARTERLIES show the correct use of braid trimmings whenever they are in style.

Sewing on flat or tubular braid—These braids are sewed from right to left. Fasten the braid on the right and hold it down ahead of you on the line where it is to be sewed. Bring the needle up so that it catches the lower edge of the braid close to

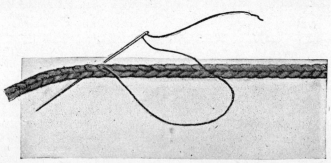

361—Sewing on flat or tubular braid

the edge, insert the needle in the material as close to where you brought it out as possible. Take a slanting stitch about ⅜ of an inch long, bringing the needle out through both the material and braid close to the upper edge. Insert the needle in the material close to where you brought it out and take another slanting stitch ⅜ of an inch long, bringing the needle out through both the material and braid close to the lower edge.   (Illustration 361.)

A narrow braid is often used near an edge on dresses to hold the hem or facing.   Flat braids are often applied by machine.

Sewing soutache braid—There are two ways of sewing on soutache braid.   The simpler is to hold the braid flat over the line of the transfer and sew through the center of the soutache, taking a very short stitch on the right side and quite a long one on the under side.   (Illustration 362.)   Or sew by machine, using the braiding attachment.

In using a design with a great many sharp turns it is better to sew the soutache so that it stands upright.   (Illustration 363.)   Hold the braid ahead of you over the line of the transfer as before, but hold the soutache upright instead of flat.   Fasten the braid securely at the right and bring the needle up through the material, just catching the lower edge of the braid.   Insert the needle as near as possible to where you brought it out, and take a stitch ¼ of an inch long.   Bring the needle out through the material, catching the lower edge of the braid.   (Illustration 363.)

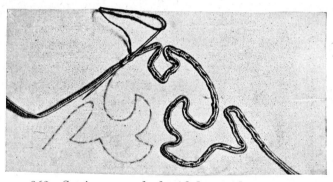

362—Sewing soutache braid flat on the material

363—Sewing soutache braid in an upright position

Sewing rickrack braid to an edge—Turn under the ⅜-inch seam allowance on the edge to form a narrow hem. Baste the braid flat on the outside of the garment, letting the points extend ⅛ inch beyond the edge. Stitch through the center of the braid, catching the hem.

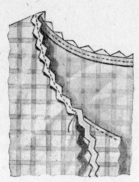

364—Sewing rickrack braid to an edge

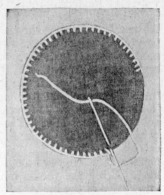

365—Blanket-stitching an appliqué circle

366—Attaching an appliqué motif with running stitches

367—Felling the edge of an appliqué motif

Appliqué

Shaped pieces of contrasting color can be appliquéd on dresses and other garments as a trimming. Usually the pieces are of the same material but in different color, but in some cases you can also use contrasting materials.

Some of the garments which are trimmed with squares, diamonds and circles of a contrasting material have a little embroidered motif in the center of each applied piece.

Cut the pieces in any shape and size that you fancy and turn under the edges ⅛ of an inch. Be very careful not to stretch them. Baste them to the garment. The edges may be blanket-stitched to the garment (Illustration 365), fastened with small running stitches (Illustration 366) or felled down (Illustration 367). The blanket-stitching takes the most time but it is also the most effective. Appliqué is often stitched by machine, and effective finishes may be obtained by making several rows of stitching, using silk or cotton of contrasting or harmonious colors.

Ostrich

Sewing on ostrich—Mark with sewing silk the line where the ostrich is to be sewed. If the ostrich has a fine cord at the upper edge, rip the cord off. Arrange the upper edge of the ostrich trimming along the thread line. Sew to position, using thread of the same color as the ostrich to make the sewing invisible.

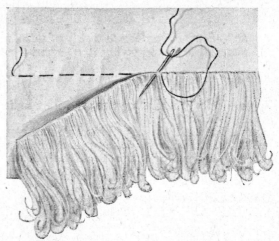

368—Sewing on ostrich trimming

Marabou

Sewing on marabou—The marabou must be sewed to a double strip of very thin material the color of the marabou. You can use China silk or fine lawn. The width of the strip should be regulated by the width of the marabou. Three-fourths or one-half

inch is about right when folded.   Fold the strip of material lengthwise with the edges lapping just a little.   Lay the marabou flat on
the table with the least attractive side uppermost.   There is always
one side that is a little better than the other.   Be sure the marabou
is flat and that there is no twist to it.   Lay the strip over the stem
of the marabou with its raw edges next the stem.   Pin it in place
at intervals and then sew it with stitches about ½ inch long.
(Illustration 369.)   Take two stitches in each place so that they
will hold firmly.

In sewing the marabou to the garment sew both edges of the strip
with running stitches.   The strip enables you to handle the marabou easily and keep it even, and prevents it from twisting.

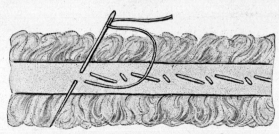

*369—Sewing marabou to a strip of thin
material before applying to a garment*

Fur

Handling fur—Pelts should always be cut with a knife from the
wrong side so as not to cut the hair.

Joinings should be made so that all the hair runs one way.

Fur should be sewed with an ordinary short needle and strong
cotton thread.   Number 30 cotton is about the right weight.

Lay the pelts edge to edge with the fur side down and sew the
edges together with an overhand stitch.   Be careful to sew
through the pelts only, without catching the hair in the sewing.
The hair can be pushed through to the right side with the needle
and after the sewing is finished the fur can be brushed gently to
make the hair lie smooth.   In this way you will conceal any sign
of the joining.

After the joining is made you will find on the wrong wide a ridge-
like seam.   This seam should be dampened and the fur should be
stretched out smooth on a flat board and tacked to it.

The fur should be left on the board until it is thoroughly dry,
which generally takes about twenty-four hours.   In the short-
haired furs the hair side of the pelt can be laid next to the board,
but in heavier furs the pelt is laid face down.

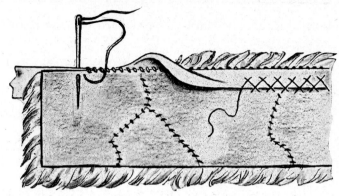

370—Finishing the edges of fur with braid or seam binding

Sewing on fur—In most cases the edges of fur must be finished with braid or seam binding the color of the fur. Overhand the edge of the braid or seam binding to the edge of the fur (Illustration 370), turn it over the edge of the fur and catch-stitch it to the pelt as illustrated. Sew it on to the garment through the braid or seam binding, using a slip-stitch.

This is the best way to handle most furs. In the case of a fur in which the pelt is not the same color as the fur itself, as in undyed furs, the binding is absolutely necessary.

When the pelt is the same color as the fur, as in dyed furs or in white furs, and the hair is long enough to cover the edge of the pelt nicely, this braid or seam binding may be omitted and the sewing done right through the pelt. In this case sew the edge of the pelt to the material with a hemming stitch. This is of course a simpler method and it is the best method to use in sewing fur to transparent materials, for the binding or braid adds to the weight of the fur.

Chapter XXIII

TURNING THE LOWER EDGE OF A GARMENT

T HE lower edge line of a garment has much to do with its smartness. The correct length varies with the fashion. The wrong length can destroy the style effect. As in most fashions, there is usually an extreme as well as a conservative version of style length. It rests with the individual to choose what suits her taste and is becoming to her figure. In planning the length of a garment, it is best to allow about an inch for the give and take of making. For this reason and owing to differences in figures, it is necessary to turn the lower edge on the person who is to wear the garment. This should not be done until the sleeves are in and the rest of the garment all ready for finishing.

Turning the Lower Edge

When a Garment is Entirely or Partly Circular, or Need Not Be Kept on the Grain of the Material at the Lower Edge

A circular skirt, flounce or godet, being cut on the bias, will always stretch more or less. It stretches because its own weight draws it down. You should make it stretch before turning the lower edge so that it will not stretch after the edge is finished.

Baste the garment together and hang it up on a hanger (Illustration 371), or on your dress form if it is not in use at the time, and let it hang for two or three days at least. At the end of that time, if the circular part of the garment extends only part way around, as in a godet, rip the seams that have bias edges while the garment is still hanging and let the bias edge drop as much as it will below the edge it was basted to. Do not pull it or force it, but let it fall naturally. Mark the amount it has stretched and rebaste it to position. Then you can turn up the lower edge.

If You Have Some One to Help You

When skirts are very short, use an 18-inch ruler or a yardstick, and, lest the eyes become confused with the various marks, paste a strip of paper on the ruler at the distance at which you want the garment to clear the floor. The paper can be of any color

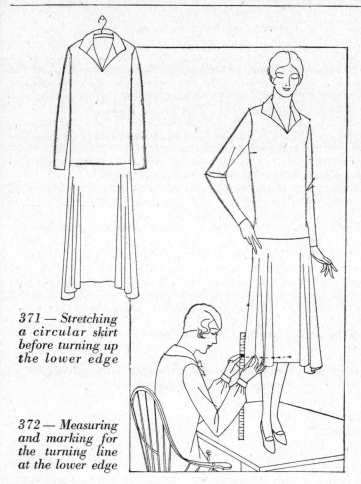

*371 — Stretching
a circular skirt
before turning up
the lower edge*

*372 — Measuring
and marking for
the turning line
at the lower edge*

which will stand out or contrast with the color of the garment. Or
you can use one of the gages that can be bought for measuring hems.

Put the garment on and, standing on a table, have some one
measure the correct length and mark the line with pins or tailors'
chalk. (Illustration 372.) Take the garment off, turn it up at
the line and baste it. Try it on again to be sure that the lower
edge is perfectly even before finishing it.

When skirts are not very short, a strip of cardboard two inches
wide and ten or twelve inches long may be used instead of the
ruler. Make a notch on one long edge at the distance at which you
want the garment to clear the floor.

If You Have No One to Help You

There are two ways of turning a lower edge when you have no one to help you. One is to take a yardstick or any straight flat stick long enough to reach from the floor to a line on the garment which you can reach easily without bending. Just below the fullest part of the hips is the best point. Stand in front of the mirror and, with the stick upright on the floor, one end touching your figure, place a pin where the top of the stick touches the garment. Move the stick around the figure a few inches at a time, marking the garment at each point. Take off the garment and measure from the pins down to the correct length.

To determine the correct length, subtract from the total length of the stick the number of inches you want the garment to clear the floor and measure down the difference. For instance, if you are using a yardstick and want your skirt to be ten inches from the ground, measure twenty-six inches from the line of pins. Mark the correct length with pins. Turn it up, baste it and try it on.

Instead of using a stick, you could make use of a dressing-table or any other piece of furniture with a flat edge of a height that comes to the right point, just below the hip. Stand against the edge of the table and mark the garment where the table touches it, turning slowly till you have marked all around. Then measure down the correct length as described before.

Adjusting the Length of a Garment with a Straight Lower Edge

If the length is to be altered the same amount all the way around, the alteration can be made at the lower edge. If it hangs unevenly and must be altered more at some places than at others, alteration must be made at the top in order not to lose the straight grain of the lower edge.

Garments with Tucks

If a straight garment has tucks, they should be put in before adjusting the length.

If a garment has tucks and does not follow the grain of the material at the lower edge, find out the amount to be taken up by the tucks and add that amount, in cutting, to the length of the garment. Then stand on a footstool or pile of books tall enough to allow the entire garment length, including the allowance for tucks, to hang straight. The lower edge can then be turned, following the directions given.

Chapter XXIV

COAT-MAKING

THE INTERLINING—Most coats require more or less interlining. The kind of material and the amount used vary
with the type of the coat and with the current styles. The
Deltor will tell you the right kind of interlining to use, and where
to place it for each pattern. This interlining *is not used for warmth*,
but to give the material sufficient body at certain places as called
for by the prevailing fashion. The method of using an additional
interlining for warmth is described further on.

All interlinings should be shrunken before they are used. If the
interlining is not shrunken beforehand, it will shrink on the first
damp day and will draw in and wrinkle the coat. The interlining
should be cut by the coat pattern, following the instructions given
in the Deltor. Baste the interlining to the wrong side of the coat,
following the Deltor. Careful basting and plenty of it are essential to successful coat-making. The importance of basting can not
be overestimated in this work. It is one of the vital points in coat-
making.

The Strictly Tailored Collar

A strictly tailored collar should have a bias interlining of the
material suggested for the purpose in the Deltor of the coat pattern
you are using. Interlinings change with the fashion, and in order
to get the correct style effect it is very necessary to use just the
material the Deltor suggests.

The interlining should be shrunken before it is used. Use the
collar pattern as a guide in cutting the interlining, but cut the interlining three-eighths of an inch smaller at all edges than the
pattern. Baste to the upper side of the collar. The "stand" of
the collar—the part next the neck, which stands up when the coat
is worn—is marked on the pattern by perforations. Roll the collar
at the perforations.

Padding-Stitches—The interlining and cloth of the collar and of the
lapels or revers on the front of the coat must be held firmly together
by many small stitches called "padding-stitches." (Illustration 373.)
These stitches are about three-quarters of an inch long on the

interlining side and just barely caught through on the right side.
Hold the collar or lapel firmly over the hand, the interlining side
uppermost and, in stitching, roll and shape the section in the
direction in which it is to lie.   (Illustration 373.)   The stitch should
be started at the line of the fold of the lapel or collar and worked in
successive rows to the edge.   The edges should be turned under,
caught to the interlining and pressed.

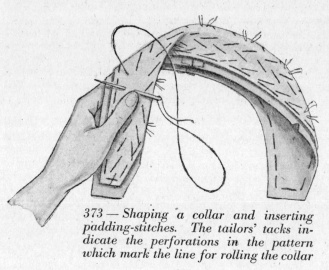

*373 — Shaping a collar and inserting
padding-stitches.   The tailors' tacks indicate the perforations in the pattern
which mark the line for rolling the collar*

After the padding-stitches are in the collar and the revers, baste
the collar, interlining side up, flat on the coat according to the
notches in the collar and in the neck.   (Illustration 374.)   Stretch
the neck edge of the collar between the notches so that it will set
smoothly on the coat.   The upper or turn-over part of the collar
must lie flat, joining the turned-over lapels of the fronts, to form
the notched collar.

When the coat has advanced thus far, try it on.   Fold over the
lapel corners of the fronts and see that the collar is the correct size
and fits properly.   If it does not, it may be shaped by shrinking or
stretching and pressing.   The front edges of the coat should lie
close to the figure at the bust and a well-fitted coat should hold
itself in shape to the figure at this point, even when unbuttoned.
If the coat is inclined to flare away at the front line, pin one or two
small dart-like tucks in the interlining about one-quarter of an inch
wide at the coat's edge and running to nothing about two inches
inside the edge.   This will shape in the edge and take out the
stretched appearance.   Mark these tucks with chalk, remove the
pins and slash the interlining at each chalk mark.   Lap the inter-

lining the same space that the tucks were made, cut away one edge to meet the other, lay a piece of cambric over the slash and sew the cambric to hold it to shape. The cloth will have the fulness that has been taken out of the interlining and must be gathered on a thread, dampened and shrunk out with the iron. Cut away the interlining to within ⅜ inch of the front edges of the coat. Cut the hem allowance from the bottom of the interlining.

On a coat that is sometimes worn rolled high, there should be no padding-stitches in the revers, as they would show when the coat is worn with the collar turned up.

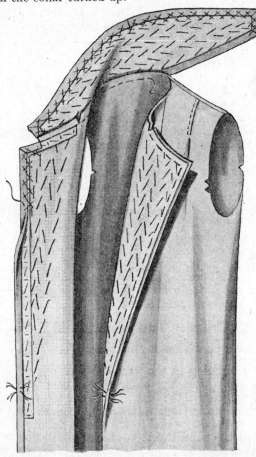

374—*A strictly tailored coat showing padding-stitches and tailors' tacks with taping on the edge of the interlining*

Taping the Edges

Narrow linen tape or the selvedge of the lining material, well shrunken, should be sewed to the interlining at the edges of the lapel and front of the coat, as far as the Deltor suggests, to hold them in shape. (Illustration 374.) Turn the edges of the coat over on the interlining and catch-stitch them. Press the fronts carefully.

Facing for a Strictly Tailored Collar and Front
Or for Any Coat with a Collar Which Is Never Worn High

Cut facings for the collar and fronts from the coat pattern and join the collar facing to the front facings, following the instructions in the Deltor. Press the seams open and baste the facing to the collar and to the front of the coat, holding the front and lapel in to their proper shape and turning in the edges of the facing. (Illustration 375.) Baste the free edges of the facing in place, being careful to allow sufficient ease for the roll. Slip-stitch or fell the edges to position.

This method of putting on a facing gives the necessary ease or extra size in the facing of both collar and revers, so neither will ever roll up on account of the facing being tight.

Collar facings of velvet are sometimes used, but instead of being applied directly over the interlining the edges of the velvet are turned under and catch-stitched to the under side of the cloth collar. One-eighth of a yard of velvet cut on the bias is usually enough for a collar facing. All pressing and shaping of the collar must be done before putting on the velvet facing.

The shawl-collar facing is sometimes cut in one with the front facing. Cut the collar and join it to the body of the coat as just described; then press it. Join the two facing sections at the back and press the seam open. Pin the facing in position. Turn in the outer edge of the facing even with the fold edge of the coat and baste, and finish as described above.

Cloth Collar in Two Sections and Facing
For a Coat That Is Sometimes Worn High

Baste the interlining to the wrong side of one collar section. (Illustration 376.) Join the collar to the coat with the seam toward the wrong side of the coat. Baste and stitch the other collar section to the facing (Illustration 377), steam or press the seam open. Arrange the collar and facing on the outside of the coat. Carefully baste the edges together, stitch (Illustration 378), press or steam the seam open. Turn the collar and facing to the inside of the coat, carefully baste to position with the seam in the edge. Turn in the lower edge of the facing and slip-stitch it to position.

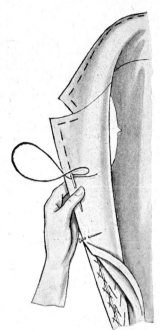

376—Basting interlining to one part of a cloth collar in two sections

375—Applying a facing to the collar and front of a strictly tailored coat

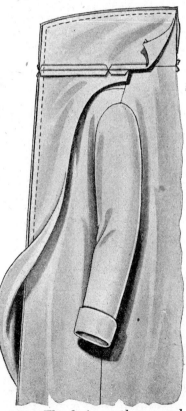

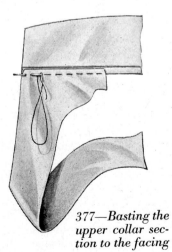

377—Basting the upper collar section to the facing

378—The facing and upper collar section stitched to the front and under collar section on a coat that is sometimes worn high

Cloth Collar in One Piece

Or a Collar That Has One or Both Sides of Fur, and a Facing for a Coat That Is Sometimes Worn High

Facing—It is best to put the facing on the coat first. Arrange the facing on the outside of the coat. Carefully baste the edges together, stitch and press or steam the seam open. Turn the facing to the inside of the coat. Baste it to position with the seam in the edge. Turn in the lower edge of the facing and slip-stitch.

Cloth collar in one piece—Baste the interlining to the wrong side of the collar. Catch the interlining to the collar invisibly with a long stitch through the center. (Illustration 379.) Fold the collar in half and stitch the ends together. (Illustration 380.) Turn right side out. Catch the interlining together with long, loose stitches. (Illustration 381.) Baste and stitch one edge of the collar to the neck. Steam or press the seam up. (Illustration 382.) Slip-stitch the free edge of the collar to the neck after the coat has been lined.

379—Interlining a cloth collar in one piece

380—Stitching the ends of the collar

381—Catching the interlining together

382—Attaching the collar to the coat

*383—Applying interlining to the cloth
section of a collar with one side of fur*

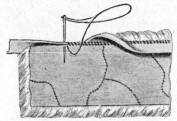

*384—Overhanding a tape to
the edge of the fur section.*

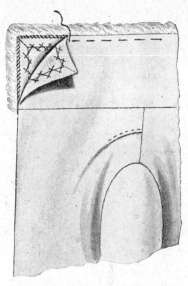

*385—Catch-stitching the tape
to the interlining of the fur*

*386—Basting the cloth section
of the collar to the fur section*

Collar with one side of fur—Baste the interlining to the cloth
section of the collar.   Trim away the outer edges of the interlining
⅜ inch.   Turn the edges of the collar over the interlining.   Catch-
stitch.   (Illustration 383.)   Baste and stitch the collar to the neck.
Steam or press the seam up.   To join the fur, lay the pelts edge to
edge, fur side down.   Overhand the edges together—do not catch
the hair in sewing.   Overhand a tape the same color to the edges.
(Illustration 384.)   Interline according to instructions given in the
Deltor of the pattern you are using.   Turn the tape over the interlining and catch-stitch.   (Illustration 385.)   Baste the cloth section to the edges of the fur collar.   (Illustration 386.)   Slip-stitch
the outer edges to position.

Collar with both sides of fur—Catch the interlining together with long, loose stitches. (Illustration 387.) Baste and slip-stitch one edge of the collar to the neck edges of the coat. (Illustration 388.) Slip-stitch the free edge of the collar to the neck after the coat has been lined.

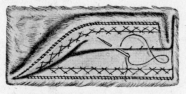

387—Catching the interlining together in a collar with both sides of fur

388 — Basting the collar to the neck edge of a coat that is sometimes worn high

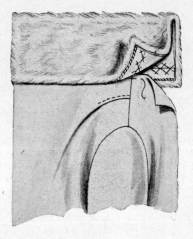

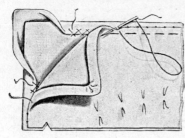

389—Turning the upper section over the interlining and applying the under section on a collar that is rolled but not tailored

Coat Collar Which Is Rolled But Not Tailored

And Is Never Worn Open

Cut an interlining, using the collar pattern as a guide. The Deltor of the coat pattern you are using will tell you what material to use for the interlining. Trim off the seam allowance on the edges that are not to be joined to the neck. Baste the interlining to the upper section of the collar. Turn the outer edge and ends of the collar over on the interlining and catch-stitch them. (Illustration 389.) Turn under the edges of the under section of the collar one-eighth of an inch more than you turned under the edges of the upper section and baste it to the upper section one-eighth inch from the edges. (Illustration 389.) Catch the under section to the interlining about three-quarters of an inch from the outer edges and also

at the line where the collar rolls over. Fell the edges to position.
(Illustration 389.) Baste the collar flat inside the neck edge of
the coat and fell the coat to the collar.

Cuff with Open Ends

Cut the interlining like the cuff pattern. Trim off the seam allowance of the upper edge and ends. Baste the interlining to the
outer section of the cuff, turn the cuff edges over the interlining,
and catch-stitch them. (Illustration 390.) Turn under the upper
edge and ends of the under section of the cuff one-eighth of an inch
more than the upper section. Baste it with its edge one-eighth of
an inch from the edge of the outer section and fell the edges to
position. (Illustration 390.) Put the cuff on the sleeve, following
the instructions given in the Deltor of the pattern you are using.

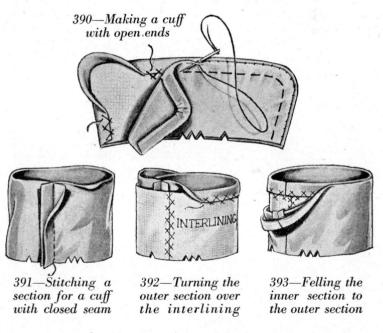

390—Making a cuff
with open ends

391—Stitching a
section for a cuff
with closed seam

392—Turning the
outer section over
the interlining

393—Felling the
inner section to
the outer section

Cuff with Closed Seam

Stitch the seam in sections (Illustration 391), stitching the seam
in the under section ⅛ inch deeper than in the upper. Steam or
press open. Cut the interlining like the cuff, trimming off ⅜-inch
seam allowance on the upper edge. Lap and catch-stitch the

ends.   (Illustration 392.)   Turn the edge of the outer section over
the interlining and catch-stitch.   (Illustration 392.)   Turn under
the top of the under section ⅛ inch more than the upper section.
Baste and fell to the upper section ⅛ inch from edge.   (Illustration 393.)

Interlining in a Sleeve When a Cuff Is Not Used

A bias strip of interlining should be basted into the wrist just
above the turning line of the hem part and the cloth turned over
and catch-stitched to it.   (Illustration 394.)

Distributing Fulness at the Top of a Coat Sleeve

There is usually more or less ease in the top of a coat sleeve.
This should be distributed as best fits the figure of the person for
whom the coat is being made.   To shrink out the fulness at the top,
slip the sleeve over the small end of a tailors' cushion.   For wools,
lay a damp cloth over the gathers and press carefully.   (Illustration
395.)   In silks, use a dry cloth and press with a warm iron.

Weights

Flat lead weights are often tacked into the bottom of a coat to
weight it properly.   They should be covered with the lining material so they will not wear through the lining and should be placed
as advised in the Deltor of the pattern you are using.

Interlining for Warmth

An additional interlining, if required for warmth, is made of
outing flannel or any of the interlinings that come for the purpose.
(Illustration 396.)   Cut it with the pattern of the coat as a guide
and follow the instructions given in the Deltor.   If only the
body of the coat is interlined, let the interlining extend an inch
or two below the waistline.   (Illustration 396.)   Slash it at intervals along the bottom so it will not bind the coat.   Do not put the
interlining together with ordinary seams but tack it inside the coat,
letting one seam edge of the interlining overlap the other.
If the sleeves are to be interlined, the interlining should be
tacked to the sleeve lining.   It is used on the upper part of the
sleeve only and should stop three inches below the upper edge and
three inches above the wrist edge.   (Illustration 397.)

Lining a Coat

The lining is the final step of coat-making.   The outside must be
entirely finished, the pockets put in and all the ornamental stitching done before beginning on the lining.

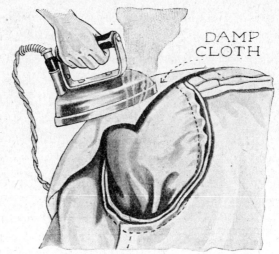

DAMP CLOTH

394—A sleeve that has no cuff

395—Shrinking out fulness at the top of a sleeve

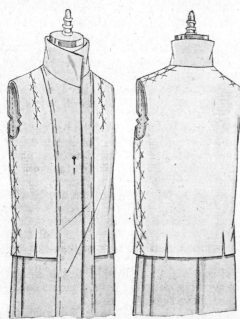

396—The correct method of putting in an interlining for warmth

397—The interlining applied to the upper part of the sleeve

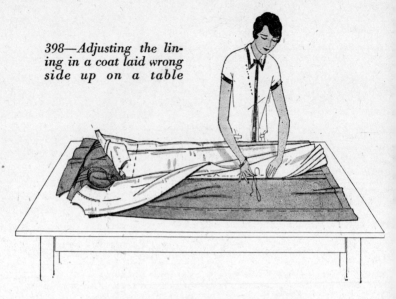

*398—Adjusting the lin-
ing in a coat laid wrong
side up on a table*

Lining a Coat That Has a Facing

Most coats have a facing.   The lining should be cut by the coat
pattern, following the instructions given in the Deltor.   Stitch the
underarm seams and press as instructed in the Deltor.

The lining must be easy in width as well as length.   If it is tight,
it will draw the outside of coat and make wrinkles—if it is short,
it will pull the coat up.

Lay the coat on the table wrong side up with the back smooth
from the armholes to the lower edge—place the lining on the
coat, wrong sides and underarm seams together.   Starting at the
armhole pin the underarm seams of the lining to the seams of the
coat with the lining slightly eased on the coat.   Sew to position
with basting stitches about ½ or ¾ inch long with a backstitch
at about every three basting stitches—leave the three basting
stitches with a little length in them so there is no danger of drawing the outside of the coat.   Baste the lining to the coat across
the back just below the armhole and about 5 or 6 inches from
the lower edge.

Smooth out the front of coat and lining, and baste the lining to
the coat across below the armhole, down the front 2 inches back of
the facing and 5 or 6 inches above the lower edge.

If you have a dress form, put the coat on the form, lining side out.
Smooth the front lining over the coat, armhole edges even, and sew
the shoulder edge to the seam of the coat in the same way as the

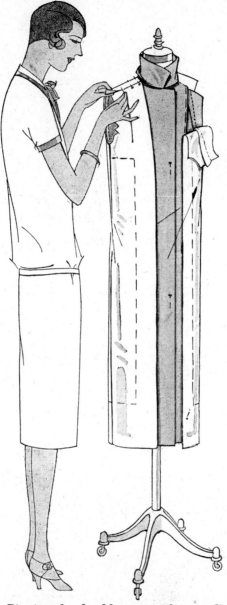

399—*Pinning the shoulder seam of a coat lining with the coat wrong side out on a dress form*

underarm seams were sewed. Smooth the back lining over the coat, with armhole edges even, turn in the shoulder edges and baste over the front. Sew the armhole and the neck edge of the lining to the coat with basting stitches about ¼ inch long. Baste the front lining to the front about 2 inches back of the facing. Turn in all outer edges and finish as instructed in the Deltor. If you have no dress form, all this work can be done on the table.

The sleeve lining is cut from the coat sleeve pattern, the seams stitched and pressed as instructed in the Deltor. Turn both sleeve and lining wrong side out. Tack the seam of the lining, if a one-seam sleeve, or the outside (back) seam, if a two-seam sleeve, to the corresponding seam of the coat sleeve the same way the under-arm seams were tacked. Slip your hand through the sleeve and turn it right side out. Slip your hand inside the lining and smooth it out. Baste sleeve and lining together four or five inches from the wrist and again four or five inches from the top. Turn in the upper and lower edges and finish as instructed in the Deltor.

Lining a Coat that Has No Facing

Some coats have no facing and the lining extends to the front edge; some are part lined; some are unlined. For these, it is best to follow the instructions given in the Deltor of the coat pattern you are using.

Fabric Fur or Fur Coats

If a coat is made of fabric fur, the entire coat should be lined with soft cambric before the interlining is put in. The cambric reen-forces and strengthens the rather loose weave of the fur cloth. It is also used in fur coats if the pelts are tender and perishable.

Coats for Girls and Children

The principles and general rules for making coats for girls and children are exactly the same as for coats for women. They are applied to the simpler form of coat used for girls and children.

Capes

Capes are made by the same general principles and rules that are followed in making coats. The effect of a cape is softer than that of a coat and in applying the principles keep the idea in mind that the cape should be as soft as required by the design of the cape. It is best to follow the instructions given in the Deltor with each Butterick cape pattern.

Chapter XXV

MATERNITY CLOTHES

Dresses—Materials—Colors—Coats—Capes—Brassière—Corsets—
Shoes—Lingerie and Underwear

MATERNITY clothes have two objects: One is to make
your condition unnoticeable, the other is to give you every
physical advantage possible. If your clothes make you feel
conspicuous and awkward, you will shrink from going out and will
suffer from lack of exercise and legitimate amusement which would
keep you in a happy, contented frame of mind.

Your clothes must be the right weight so that they will not tire
or strain you. They must be the right size so that they give your
figure proper support without compressing it or retarding its development.

Clothes that are designed solely for maternity wear are apt to
look the part and call attention to a woman's condition. At this
time you do not want to be conspicuous in any way. You want to
look as much like other women as possible so that there will be
nothing to draw notice to you. It is much better to choose current
styles that can be adapted to maternity wear and use them in preference to the special maternity clothes. Your things will be
prettier and smarter and of more use to you later. The slight alterations that you make for maternity use can be changed back to
normal lines after the baby is born.

You should avoid anything that is extreme or bizarre or that will
enlarge your figure unnecessarily. Dresses with plaits or soft fulness are admirable, for they give you the size you need at the
waist. You should not wear a dress that is extremely narrow. It
might become too small for you before the baby is born. If you
select such a style, it is advisable to add sufficient width to it in
cutting. Surplice styles, especially when they are made with
sashes, adapt themselves to your changing figure with the tying of
the sash.

Materials and colors—It is advisable to choose materials that are
light in weight, especially for coats and street dresses. As far as
possible wear the light-weight materials even in winter in your
dresses. Get the necessary warmth from your underwear and
your wraps. Coats and wraps, of course, must be warm for cold

weather, but you can choose materials that are warm and yet light.

Do not choose loud or light colors for outdoor-garment use. The quiet colors are less noticeable and the dark colors make you look small. Avoid anything with large figures or conspicuous stripes, checks or plaids. In summer you will want to wear white and light colors during hot weather, because they are cooler than dark colors, but in other seasons the dark colors are more practical for the street. Use light colors for the house.

Coats, capes—For the street a long coat or a cape is best for maternity wear. The coat should not be close fitting. It should have plenty of width at the waistline.

Brassière—You should wear a brassière that supports your figure and keeps it neat and trim. A brassière should not be worn at all snug, for it must not compress the figure or prevent its development. Surplice brassières are excellent, for they adjust themselves each time they are put on. Or you can use the fitted brassière with underarm seams laced with elastic cord which can be let out when necessary.

Corsets—As soon as you find that you need them, get the best maternity corsets that you can afford and be sure to wear hose supporters. A round garter is not desirable, for it checks the circulation and might induce varicose veins.

Shoes—Your shoes should have flat, rather low heels so that you will not run the risk of turning your ankles and getting a fall. In wet or slippery weather be sure to wear rubbers.

Lingerie and underwear—For maternity wear you will probably need lingerie at least two sizes larger than the underwear you ordinarily use. Instead of petticoats it is advisable to wear princess slips, for the weight rests on the shoulders instead of at the waistline. If you use envelope chemises, you must allow extra length in the lower part in cutting them.

Slash the pattern just below the hip and separate the pieces about three inches before you cut your material. Also, allow three inches additional on the tab in cutting. Nightgowns should open down the front.

You should place yourself under the care of a good physician as soon as possible and follow his advice in regard to exercise, diet, etc.

Chapter XXVI

THE LAYETTE

A LL baby clothes should be white, and as fine and dainty as possible. Pale shades of baby pink and blue can be used for ribbons on dresses and caps, for linings in lingerie caps and for the linings of summer coats of batiste, handkerchief linen and crêpe de Chine.

Pale pink and blue are also used for baby kimonos, sacks, sweaters and bootees, and for afghans, blankets, etc. But the actual dresses, slips, caps and coats, petticoats, etc., are always white.

A little baby must be kept absolutely clean, warm and dry.

The layette given below is complete and large enough to keep a baby fresh and dainty if one can have constant laundry work done. It is, however, the smallest layette that is safe to start with, and it would be desirable to enlarge it, especially in the matter of diapers, bands and shirts. You must have at least:

3 Dresses	3 Knitted Shirts
3 Nightgowns	3 Knitted Bands
3 Petticoats	3 Flannel Bands
3 Bibs	3 Pairs of Bootees
3 Kimonos	24 Diapers 18 x 18 ins.
3 Sacks	6 Quilted Pads 11 x 16 ins.

The baby will need a coat and cap. These things should, however, be left until the last, for you are very apt to receive them as presents.

You will find an excellent collection of babies' garments in the Butterick publications and very exquisite French designs for embroidering them.

For materials it is best to rely on the list printed on the back of every Butterick pattern envelope. The nicest baby clothes are made entirely by hand. Machine-work is of course more quickly done. The simplest and best way to make each little garment is explained and pictured in the Deltor enclosed in the pattern envelope.

A Deltor also shows in pictures the easiest and best way to dress the baby—just how to handle the little body, tiny hands and feet in the easiest, most comfortable and quickest way for both the baby and its mother.

Chapter XXVII

BOYS' AND MEN'S CLOTHES

Patterns—Alterations—Materials—Cutting—Putting the Garment Together—
Trousers—The Fly—Trousers for Smaller Boys—Trousers with No Fly—
Blouses or Coats—Strictly Tailored Coat—Canvas Lapels—Front Edges—
Facing—Seams—Lining—Collar—Shirts—Bathrobes—House Jackets—Undergarments

I T IS not difficult to make garments for boys and men. It is mainly a matter of correct finish and careful pressing with hot irons, whenever pressing is necessary. The frequent use of irons is a very important part of tailoring.

It is essential to get the right-size patterns. The proper way to measure men and boys is given on pages 14-16.

Alterations

If it is necessary to make any alterations in the length of a pattern, they should be made before cutting your material. The Deltor will tell you where to make them.

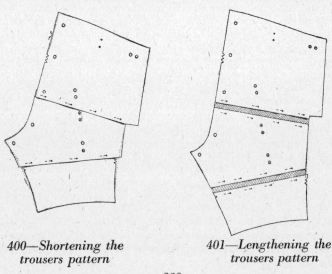

400—Shortening the
trousers pattern

401—Lengthening the
trousers pattern

To shorten or lengthen the trousers considerable care is needed in determining just where the alteration should be made. In the case of small boys where the trousers are buttoned to an underwaist, the length of the underwaist has a great deal to do with their length when worn.

It is well to measure an old pair of trousers on the tissue, taking the measure from the waist to the crotch and then to just above the knee, allowing for the extra fulness to fall over the knee in knickerbockers.

Any alteration in length above the crotch should be made across the pattern below the extension for the pocket opening, changing the seam edges as little as possible. In the lower leg part, fold the plait across or slash in line with the notches. (Illustrations 400 and 401.)

Materials

Before cutting your material read page 26 "Quality in Materials," pages 54-70 "Making Your Garment," and pages 237-242 "Pressing, Sponging and Shrinking."

Cutting

After the material has been properly sponged or otherwise shrunken lay the pattern on it as shown in the Deltor layout of the pattern you are using. Use plenty of pins in pinning the pattern on the material and cut with sharp shears, following the edge of the pattern exactly.

Mark all the working perforations with tailors' tacks (pages 91-92) and either mark the notches with two or three stitches in basting cotton or clip them, making the clips no deeper than is necessary to see them distinctly.

Putting the Garment Together

Follow the Deltor for putting the pieces of the garment together. (See Chapter XIV, page 120, for pockets.)

Trousers with Fly Closing

Baste a facing of lining material, cut from the fly pattern, to the outside of the front edge of the left portion. Stitch the seam. Turn the facing to the inside, and baste it flat, with the cloth at the seam edge entirely covering the lining.

Now lay together, face to face, two fly pieces, one of cloth and one of lining, and stitch the seam on the front edge. Turn it to the right side, baste flat and press.

Make the buttonholes in the fly. They are worked from the cloth side, the first one coming just below the waistband. Then baste the fly into position, its edge a trifle back of the edge on the left front. Stitch ⅜ inch back of the buttonholes, through the four thicknesses of goods, down from the waistband, ending in a curved line at the lower edge. (Illustration 402.) Tack the fly between the buttonholes to the facing. Overcast the raw edges on the inside.

The underlapping fly piece for the buttons on the right front should be interlined with canvas and faced with lining. Baste and stitch the cloth piece to the edge of the right front of the trou-

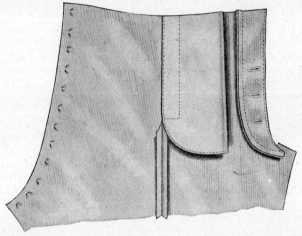

402—The inside finish of trousers with a fly closing

sers and press the seam open. Turn under the lining, clipping the edge to make it lie flat, and baste it to the cloth seam. From the right side stitch neatly an even line down close to the basting and across the free edge at the bottom.

Sew small buttons in position corresponding to the buttonholes on the opposite fly.

For the smaller boy, when buttons and buttonholes are impracticable, the small facing provided for in the pattern is attached to the outside of both of the fronts, stitched and turned to the inside. (Illustration 404.) The front seam is then closed from the facing to the waistline. The side pockets should be put in next.

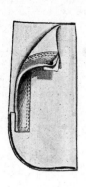
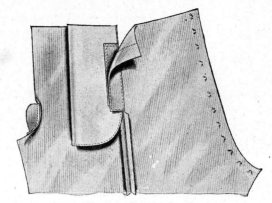

403—A side pocket   404—The inside finish of trousers
  for trousers   without a fly closing

Side pockets of trousers are usually made in a seam. Cut a square
piece of silesia or stout lining material the size desired, and, doub-
ling it over, notch the edges to indicate the pocket opening. Make
corresponding notches in the seam edges of the trousers. Face the
back edge of the pocket on both the right and wrong sides with bias
facings of the cloth one inch and a quarter wide and long enough to
extend from the top of the pocket to an inch below the notch in
the opening. (Illustration 403.) Lay the front edge of the pocket
edge to edge with the front edge of the trousers on their wrong side
and baste it to them. In the same seam baste a bias facing of the
cloth to the front of the trousers on the right side. (Illustration
404.) This facing should be the same length and width as the
facings on the back edge of the pocket. Stitch the pocket, trousers
and facing together in a narrow seam. Turn the facing over on
to the pocket and run a row of stitching close to the fold to hold it
in place. Turn under the back edge of the facing and stitch it to
the pocket. Trim off the lower corners of the pocket, and crease
the edge for a seam toward the inside. The seam of the pocket
may then be closed. Baste it first, and close it with one stitching.
The back edge of the pocket is caught to the front with bar stay-
tacks. The upper edges are held by the waistband.

Trousers Having No Fly Closing

These have the waistband divided into a front and back, leaving
an opening at each side of the trousers. In this case the extension
on the side of the back pieces of the trousers is faced, thus forming
the underlap for the opening. (Illustration 404.) Now the upper

edges of the pockets are basted to the upper edge of the trousers front.   (Illustration 404.)

Make a bar, overcast or buttonholed, between the two rows of stitching, catching through the cloth and both sides of the pocket at the top and at the bottom of the opening.

Blouses or the coats of suits vary considerably in style.   It is best to rely on the Deltor of the pattern you are using for making and finishing.

A Strictly Tailored Coat for a Man or Boy

This is made in very much the same way as a strictly tailored coat for a woman except that the effect is even more tailored. The best tailors give a well-tailored and mannish look to a coat by the methods given below.

For this style of coat it is very important to know how to baste in the canvas, face the front of the coat and put in the lining before joining the shoulder seam.   Not until this has been done should the collar be basted to the coat.   These are the fine points of tailoring and should be followed closely in coat-making.

The Canvas in the Coat Front

In basting the canvas to the front of the coat the basting should not be done from the canvas side, but the coat should be placed flat on the table *over* the canvas and the two basted together from the *outside* of the coat.   This is done to prevent making the canvas too short, which would cause the coat to pucker.   -

The canvas and cloth in the lapel of the coat are held together by padding stitches.   The method of making these padding stitches is shown on page 214.   Hold the lapel over the hand with the canvas side up and start the padding stitches a little back of the crease roll at the neck and gradually taper them to the crease roll at the front of the coat.   The stitches are then worked outward to the edge of the lapel.   The canvas in the front of the coat and in the lapel is then trimmed off one-half inch from the edge

To prevent the front edges of the coat and lapel from stretching use a narrow linen or cotton tape which has been thoroughly shrunken, placing it along the front edge of the coat and of the lapel.   (Page 215, Illustration 374.)   Place the tape a good three-eighths of an inch from the edge, so that later when sewing on the facing the tape will not be caught in the facing sewing.   Also sew a tape one-eighth of an inch in back of the crease roll of the lapel, starting the tape about an inch from the front edge of the coat and extending it one inch above the neck edge. When a soft roll in the lapel is desired, the tape along the crease roll is omitted. When the tape has been sewed on carefully, the fronts are pressed and the lapels pressed back.

The Facing

The method of putting on the facing is the same as for women's coats. (Page 216.)

Turn up the hem at the bottom of the coat and turn in the bottom of the facing even with the coat and baste. Baste the back edge of the facing to the canvas and catch-stitch it. Fell the lower edge to position.

The Seams

When using a material which ravels easily, the seams should be overcast if the coat is lined. If the coat has a half or full skeleton lining, the seams should be bound. The back edge of the facing and the hem at bottom of the coat should also be bound.

The Lining

The coat is now ready for the lining. Place the coat on the table with the shoulder seams open and baste the back section of the lining to the inside of the coat with the underarm edges of the lining along the underarm seams.

Baste the fronts of the lining to the inside of the coat. Turn under the underarm edges and baste them over the back. Turn under the front edges and baste them over the facing, allowing a little ease in width. Turn under the bottom of the lining and place it one-half inch from the bottom of the coat, basting the lining to position one-half inch from the edge. After the lining has been basted in position stitch the shoulder seams of the coat and press the seams open. (Pages 237-242.) Turn to the outside of the coat and baste the shoulder seams to the canvas.

The Collar

The under section of the collar for a coat should be of undercollar cloth which can be purchased at any tailors' trimming store and comes in gray, brown, blue and black at about twelve or fifteen cents a collar. In purchasing this cloth any store of this kind has a form for a notched collar which they lay on the material and cut just the amount required for the collar. This piece of material must be sponged. (Page 241.)

Cut the under collar like the pattern. Join the back edges and press the seam open. After pressing, trim off the edges of the under collar three-eighths of an inch. Baste a piece of canvas (cut bias) over the collar and baste along the crease roll. The stand of the collar, which is the part near the neck up as far as the crease roll, should be held together with rows of machine-stitching, making the rows one-eighth of an inch apart. The turn-over part of the collar is held together by padding stitches, using the same method as in making the lapel. Press the collar into shape, stretching the bottom of the stand from three-eighths to one-half inch and the outer edge about one-quarter inch.

Fold the collar along the crease roll, canvas side up, and press it into shape. Trim off the edges of the canvas and under collar three-eighths inch all around. Baste the neck edge of the collar to the neck edge of the coat three-eighths inch from the edge and overhand the collar in place. Then turn to the inside and catch-stitch the neck edge of the coat to the collar. The upper end of the tape along the crease roll of the lapel which extends over the neck edge should be sewed to the collar inside the crease roll. This prevents the roll line at the neck from stretching.

The top of the facing should be turned in and slip-stitched along the top of the lapel and along the outline at the bottom of the collar.

The top collar should now be basted over the collar along the crease roll and about one-half inch from the outer edge, making sure that there is plenty of size in the top collar when the collar is rolled back. Turn under the edges of the top collar (except the neck edges between the shoulder seams) even with the edges of the under collar and baste. Fell the outer edges of the under collar to the collar. Slip-stitch the lower edge of the collar along the top of the facing. Baste the shoulder edge of the lining back to the seam of the coat. Turn under the shoulder edge of the lining front and baste it over the lining back. Turn under the neck edge and baste it over the collar edge.

Bathrobes, House Jackets, Undergarments, Sleeping Garments, Etc.

In making any of these garments follow the Deltor given with the pattern. Each of these types of garments should be finished according to the style and the purpose for which it is to be used. In all these garments for boys and men it is important that every detail of the work be done neatly and accurately and according to the directions given with the pattern.

Chapter XXVIII

PRESSING, SPONGING AND SHRINKING

Irons — Ironing-Board — Sleeve-Board — Tailors' Cushion — Pressing Seams—
Pressing Pile Fabrics—Steaming Velvet, Etc.—Pressing Plaits—
Sponging and Shrinking

G OOD pressing is a very important part of dressmaking and
tailoring. Special boards and tailors' cushions may be made
at home or bought from any dressmakers' supply house.

Irons

You should have either an electric iron or an ordinary iron. A
six-pound smoothing-iron is a satisfactory type for pressing.

Ironing-Board

An ironing-board should present a smooth, firm but soft surface.
It is impossible to do good pressing on a board with a surface broken by hollows or ridges, so the first essential is a smooth, hard piece
of board of the desired size and shape.

The board should be covered with at least four thicknesses of
cotton felt, which may be bought at any store that carries tailors'
and dressmakers' supplies. If this material is not available, a
good substitute is an old woolen blanket. Care should be taken,
however, not to use pieces that have holes in them, as this might
affect the evenness of the pressing surface.

How to Cover an Ironing-Board

The under covering of felt or flannel should be stretched firmly
around the board, layer by layer, and either tacked to the under
side with flat-headed tacks or sewed together so that there is no
possibility of wrinkles developing.

When enough layers have been fastened on to give the desired
softness, a final covering of unbleached muslin or other firm smooth
cotton material should be stretched over and fastened firmly.

237

Sleeve-Board

A sleeve-board which can be used for sleeves and short seams can be made from a board two or three feet long and tapering from five or six inches in width at one end to three inches at the other. (Illustration 405.)   The ends and edges should be rounded, and the board should be padded as described.

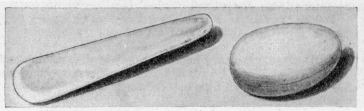

405—The sleeve-board   406—The tailors' cushion

Tailors' Cushion

A tailors' cushion is used for pressing darts and curved seams. It is ham-shaped and is stuffed tightly with cotton rags.   Cut two pieces of unbleached cotton or other firm material eighteen by fourteen inches, making them narrower at one end.   (Illustration 406.)   Round off all the edges. Stitch the seam with a close stitch.

Pressing Seams

Seams should be pressed over the tailors' cushion so that the seam edges will not be marked on the garment.   In opening seams, dampen the seam if the material will permit it and press slowly, bearing down heavily on the iron.   Very little dampness should be used on wool materials as it flattens the texture.   Little or no dampness should be used on silks.   A cloth well wrung out of water may be used on these materials when necessary and their seams may be dampened slightly.

Pressing Pile Fabrics

Velvet, plush and wool pile fabrics should not be pressed in the usual way, but they can be pressed on a wire board made especially for the purpose.   This board is made of fine wires set close together in a slanting position on a heavy canvas back which is tacked to a flat board.   The pile sinks between the wires when pressed and is not injured.   (Illustrations 407-409.)   Six by eighteen inches

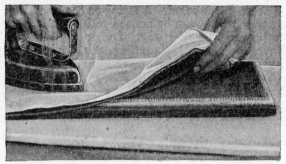

407—Pressing a pile fabric on a wire board

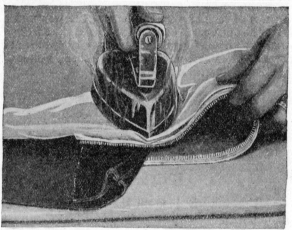

408—Pressing the edge of a garment between wires

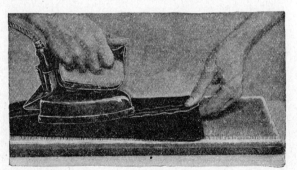

409—Pressing a seam on a wire board

is a good average-size board. A facing on the front edge of a coat of these nap materials can be pressed with seam in edge by using this wire board in another way. Loosen the tacks holding the wired canvas to the board; place the part of the material that is to be pressed on one end of the wires and fold the other end of the wired canvas over the material. Place a damp piece of muslin over the canvas and press as shown in Illustration 408.

This board is rather expensive for private use, and if it is not available it is best to steam these materials in the following way:

Steaming Velvet, Etc.

To steam velvet, etc., invert a heated iron and slip the small end of a sleeve-board through the handle. Place something under the ends of the board to hold it firmly. (Illustration 410.) Lay a damp piece of muslin over the face of the iron and draw the velvet over the muslin. The steam will have the effect of pressing velvet without hurting the pile. Seams can be opened in this way, and this method can be used on velvet, plush, velours, duvetyn and other materials with a high nap.

To "Mirror" Velvet

Velvet may be mirrored or panned by passing an iron over the surface of the velvet, ironing with the nap. After velvet has gone through this process it can be pressed as much as is necessary.

How to Press

Nearly all pressing is done on the wrong side. Suitings and heavy cloth may be pressed on the right side by steaming. Wring out a cloth as dry as possible and lay it over the place to be pressed.

410—Steaming velvet over an inverted iron

Have the irons hot and press firmly until the cloth is nearly dry. Turn the garment to the wrong side and press until thoroughly dry.

The shine which sometimes comes in pressing may be removed by placing a dry cloth over the shiny place. Then wring out as dry as possible a second cloth which has been thoroughly wet. Place it over the dry one, and with a hot iron pass lightly over the spot. If the material has a nap requiring raising, the place may be brushed with a stiff brush and the process of steaming repeated.

Many fabrics retain the imprint of the basting-thread under heavy pressing. For such material it is necessary to give a light pressing first, removing all basting-threads before the final pressing.

Pressing Plaits in a Skirt or Dress

Turn the skirt wrong side out and slip it over an ironing-board. Pin the top and bottom of the skirt to the board, taking care that the plaits lie perfectly flat underneath. In wool and cotton materials a sponge cloth may be placed over the skirt and pressed thoroughly until the cloth is dry. This method creases the material well and the plaits will stay in position for a long time.

In silk material press the plaits with an iron that is not too hot. Afterward the iron may be run under the plaits to smooth the part underneath. Slip the skirt off the board and remove the bastings.

In laundering or pressing a plaited skirt you will realize the value of shrinking the material and following the correct grain line of the weave.

When a plaited skirt is made of washable material it is not difficult to launder if one goes about it in the right way. (See page 249.)

Sponging and Shrinking

Almost all the wool materials should be sponged before they are used. Sponging shrinks the material and if it were not done before the material was made up the material would shrink the first damp day and ruin the appearance and possibly the usefulness of the garment. Sponging also prevents the ordinary spotting from rain, drops of water, etc. It is necessary protection to your material. There are, however, certain wool materials that should not be sponged; but most wool materials should be sponged either at the store where you buy them or at home. Most large shops will do the sponging for you, but it is easy to do it yourself. If you are uncertain as to whether your material should be sponged or not, experiment with a small piece of it first. If it shrinks too much or changes its appearance or color, do not sponge it.

When purchasing woolens that have not been sponged, an

allowance of about two and one-half inches to the yard should be made for skrinkage.

For sponging you will need a large table and ironing-blanket and a strip of heavy unbleached muslin the width of your material and one-half its length.

Lay your material face down on the table. Wet the muslin with cold water and wring it out. Spread it out, pulling out all the wrinkles, and lay it over half of your material. Fold the other half of the material over it, roll the material and sponging-cloth together in a tight roll and let it lie overnight covered with a piece of muslin and some newspapers so that the moisture will be retained.

In the morning unroll the material, pressing it dry on the wrong side as you unroll it. In sponging material of double width open it out its full width and sponge it in the same way, using a double width of muslin for the shrinking process.

Certain wool materials, such as deep-pile fabrics, should be steamed instead of sponged.

Any of these materials can be steamed on a wire board (see page 238). Lay a damp piece of muslin on the wrong side of the material (the right side being next to the wire board) and press (Illustration 407, page 239). Or use the same table, ironing-blanket and unbleached muslin as for sponging. Lay the material face down on the blanket as for sponging. Wet the muslin and lay it over the material as for sponging. Hold a moderately hot iron so that it just touches the material enough to let the steam go through the material. Pass it over the muslin, but do not let it rest on it or it will mark the material. It must just touch the muslin.

The heavier wash materials of the cotton and linen order should be shrunk in the same way before they are made up. Cottons shrink about one inch to the yard.

Voiles, fine mulls, organdies, swisses, etc., are not to be shrunk, for the skrinking changes them too much and they are not as pretty afterward.

Chapter XXIX

CLEANING

Woolens—Silks—Velvet—Black Lace—White Lace—Grease-Spots—Machine-Oil Stains—Blood-Stains—Ink-Stains—Iron-Rust—Fruit-Stains—Mildew—Paint—Chewing-Gum

CLEANING can frequently be done at home with very little trouble and expense. The simplest way to clean woolen goods is to wash them in warm soap-suds or with soap bark. Select any pure, mild soap in either cake or flaked form and dissolve it in hot water, whisking it into foamy suds. Then add cool water until it is barely lukewarm. Place the material in the solution and gently squeeze it between the hands or press with a vacuum cup "pouncer." Rinse in another suds or in clear water and gently squeeze out the surplus water. *Do not wring.*

To use soapbark, get ten cents' worth of soapbark and pour over it two quarts of boiling water. Let it stand until the strength is taken from the bark, strain, and pour into a tub of lukewarm water. Let the goods stand for half an hour in the suds, then rub well and rinse in another water of the same temperature.

Press on the wrong side before it is thoroughly dry. Experiment first with a small piece of the material to be sure that it does not change color or shrink badly.

Silks

For silks, mix six ounces of strained honey and four ounces of a pure soap with one pint of pure alcohol or a good substitute.

Lay each piece of silk flat on a table or marble, and with a brush cover the silk with the mixture, first on one side and then on the other. Brush the silk as little as possible and always straight up and down. Dip the silk in several tepid rinsing waters, the last one mixed with a little honey. Do not wring the silk, but hang it up, and when half-dry iron with a cool iron on the wrong side.

Black silk can be freshened by sponging with strong black coffee, or with glove-water made by boiling an old black kid glove in water for some time.

A good method of cleaning black silk is to sponge the silk on both

243

sides with one-half teaspoonful of household ammonia to a quart of water, and then iron on the wrong side with a piece of muslin between the silk and the iron.

Ribbons may be cleansed in the same way and rolled smoothly over a bottle or round stick to dry.

Velvet

Velvet is cleaned by steaming. First brush the velvet thoroughly with either a soft or stiff brush until all dust and lint are removed. It is better to use a soft brush if the velvet is not too dirty.

If a milliner's steaming-box is at hand, invert a hot iron in the box and cover the face of the iron with a good-sized piece of muslin which has been thoroughly wet. This produces steam, and the muslin must be moved along as it dries. The velvet is held with its wrong side against the muslin and brushed carefully with a soft brush until the pile of the velvet is raised. Always brush against the nap. The pile may also be raised by holding the velvet tightly over a pan of boiling water or over an inverted iron as described on page 271.

Laces

For black laces, an old-fashioned cleaning mixture is made by boiling an old black kid glove in a pint of water until half the water has evaporated. Strain, and, if necessary, add a little cold water. After brushing the lace, dip it up and down in the liquid. Then roll it over a bottle, or pin smoothly over a covered board to dry.

White lace may be washed in a suds of pure soap, then thoroughly rinsed and pinned over a covered board to dry. Some laces will stand ironing on the wrong side. Let the lace partially dry, and iron over several thicknesses of flannel.

Removing Spots

Grease-spots on woolen or silk may be removed by naphtha, gasoline, ether or chloroform.

A good mixture for removing grease-spots is made from equal parts of alcohol, benzin and ether.

These solvents are highly inflammable, and must, therefore, never be used in the same room with an open light or flame.

There are, however, a number of excellent cleaners on the market that are not inflammable.

Lay the material, right side down, on a piece of clean blotting-paper or brown wrapping-paper. Rub around and around the spot with a piece of the same material which has been dipped in the cleaning-fluid. Be careful to approach the spot gradually and keep rubbing around the edge of the spot which is damp with the cleaning-fluid so that no ring forms. If you do not approach the spot gradually, the grease will spread over a large surface. Ether and chloroform are less liable to leave a ring than gasoline or naphtha.

Grease can also be removed from silk or woolen materials by spreading French chalk over the spot and allowing it to stand for some time. This absorbs the grease. Shake the chalk off the garment and if it leaves a mark dissolve the remaining particles with benzin or ether, being careful to rub around the edge of the spot which is damp with these fluids until they have completely evaporated, to prevent a ring from forming. Powdered French chalk or Fuller's earth may be used by placing the powder over the stain and holding over a heated iron. The heat will dissolve the grease, and the powder will absorb it.

Grease can be removed from most materials by placing the material, right side down, over a piece of brown wrapping-paper and pressing over the wrong side of the material with a hot iron. The heat of the iron drives the grease from the material into the paper, because grease has a tendency to go from a warm spot to a cooler one.

To remove grease from white goods, wash with soap. Colored cottons or colored woolens may be washed with lukewarm soap lyes.

Machine-oil stains.—Washing with cold water and a pure soap will remove most stains of machine-oil. If they are especially difficult to remove, moisten borax and rub it on the stain from the outside toward the center, taking care not to spread the oil. Pour cold water through the material.

Blood stains may be taken out by washing with soap and tepid water. They may also be removed by covering the spot with wet laundry starch and allowing it to stand. Afterward it should be washed.

To remove fresh ink.—Fresh ink can be removed from almost any material by stretching it tightly over a bowl or deep vessel and pouring boiling water through the spot with force from a height. Or, if still moist, rub either salt, meal flour or sugar, and wash in cold water.

Old ink-stains can often be taken out by use of ink-eradicator which comes for that purpose. Directions for using it accompany each bottle.

In white materials squeeze lemon-juice over the spot and cover with salt. Then place the article in the sun for a while and wash.

The process may be repeated, if necessary, until the ink-spot is entirely removed.

Another method of removing ink-stains from white materials is to let the material soak in javelle water, made from one-half pound of sal soda, two ounces chlorid of lime and one quart of water. After soaking a few minutes wash in clear water.

To remove copy or India ink from white materials.—Make a strong solution of oxalic acid and cold water. Soak the spot for a few moments in the oxalic acid and then soak it in ammonia. If necessary, repeat until the stain disappears. Rinse thoroughly in cold water.

To remove fruit stains.—Make a solution of oxalic acid and water, using about ten grains of the acid to a half pint of water. Wet the article in hot water and then apply the solution of oxalic acid to the spot. Rinse it well after the spot has been removed.

To remove fruit or ink-stains.—Soak the spot for a few moments in chloroform and then soak it in very strong ammonia. Try a sample of your material first, to be sure that the chloroform and ammonia do not remove the color.

To remove iron-rust from white materials.—Lay the article in the sun and apply oxalic acid to the spot with your fingers wet with water. When the spot is removed, rinse the garment thoroughly. Also wash your hands well after using the acid. It is practically impossible to remove iron-rust from colored fabrics, as the acid used in removing the spot takes out the color so that the remedy is worse than the rust.

The javelle water and lemon-juice suggested for ink-stains may also be used to remove iron-rust.

Mildew is the hardest of all stains to remove, and can not always be taken out successfully. Salts of lemon or any of the mediums used for ink and iron-rust may be tried. *For silk only,* dip a flannel in alcohol and rub briskly, first on one side and then on the other.

Paint, when fresh, can be removed with turpentine or benzin. Or, it may be rubbed with equal parts of turpentine and alcohol. Turpentine mixed with a little ammonia is also good. Wash off with soap-suds or benzin.

To remove chewing-gum hold the under side of the garment over a hot iron until the gum is melted. Then wipe it off with a rag wet with pure alcohol or a substitute.

Chapter XXX

LAUNDERING

Colored Fabrics—Setting Colors—Restoring Faded Tints—Silk Crêpes
Chiffons—Silk Underwear—Rayon—Beaded Garments—Plaited Garments—
Circular Flares—Corduroy—Ratine or Turkish Toweling—To Prevent
Mildew—Silk Hosiery—Woolens

YOU need have no fear of ruining fine delicately colored fabrics when laundering them if you will spend one or two minutes to test the color of the material before purchasing. Despite the fact that the fabric-buying public has forced much improvement in the situation, there are unfortunately many materials marketed to-day which are not absolutely fast to washing in clear water. When buying dress material there is no way of distinguishing the fast from the non-fast colors unless the merchant is willing to guarantee them. When there is any doubt about it, it is advisable to dip a sample containing all the colors into a small dish or tumbler of lukewarm water. If the wash water is discolored, it is a good indication that the dyes are not fast to water washing. This is not a hard-and-fast rule, however, and colors which discolor the water very slightly may be washed with a fair degree of safety. Any material coloration, however, is an almost sure indication that the soap washing will prove unsuccessful.

If it is decided that the sample is not washable in water, try the old-fashioned method of setting the color. If the colors can be set in the sample, it is safe to buy the material, though it will be necessary to set the color at every washing.

If neither of these tests proves successful, better not buy the material, unless you are willing to have it dry cleaned, when necessary.

If color is fast to water, it will be found that any neutral soap will give excellent washing results. Mild neutral soaps will not injure colors which wash satisfactorily in water.

To Set Colors in Wash Materials

Different colors must be set by different methods. Green, blue, purple and also mauve or lavender can be set by soaking for a short time in alum water. Use about an ounce of alum to a gallon of water. Blue, pink and most red materials can be set by soaking in salt water, using a large tablespoonful of salt to a gallon of water.

247

To set the color in brown, tan and deep yellow, use about a cup-ful of vinegar to a gallon of water and soak the material in it. Black cotton materials and black-and-white materials may be soaked in strong salt water or a little turpentine may be added to the water.

Yellow and the lighter shades of tan can be brightened when they become faded by adding a little strong coffee to the rinsing water.

To Restore Faded Tints

When light-colored materials fade in the laundry and get that washed-out appearance that makes them look old, the freshness may be restored by using any of the good tints obtainable. These are dyes that do not require boiling. Some of them come in soap form and some are added to the rinsing water after the manner of bluing. They are easy to use and sometimes have quite lasting results so that it is not always necessary to use them each time the garment is washed.

These tints come in two varieties—one that will dye any fabric, and one that will dye silk only, leaving lace trimmings untinted.

To Wash Silk Crêpes, Chiffons, Silk Underwear, Rayon and All Fine Fabrics

Use warm water, and any soap flakes not too strong with lye. Be sure to follow the directions given with the soap flakes you use. Do not rub, but after a good suds is made dip the garment in it and squeeze the suds through the garment—wash quickly—never leave silk in the water over five minutes. Thoroughly rinse in several waters so that not one particle of soap is left on the gar-ment. Do not wring the water out, squeeze it. Shake out the article and wrap up in a soft cloth until nearly dry. Iron on the wrong side with a warm iron, never a hot one. Iron the crêpes crosswise of the material, stretching a little as you iron.

Remember Georgette crêpe or any other thin crêpe is liable to part or give way on the crosswise strands, so don't be rough with it.

Gray and bisque are many times unwashable colors. If either of these colors should change to an entirely different color during washing, one or more of the dyes used are not fast. These two colors are made by blending red, yellow and blue dyes and one or more may prove to be unwashable. Many times pleasing even shades will result if the unfast dye is completely washed out by repeated soap washings, and a fresh color may be given by the use of the tints already mentioned.

To Wash a Beaded Garment

Use the same method as for thin crêpes. Never put a beaded garment through a wringer, for it would break the beads. Lay the garment right side down on a Turkish towel or soft pressing-pad so as not to break the beads in pressing. Embroidered garments should be pressed in this way also, as the design will appear more raised and less flattened than if pressed on a hard surface.

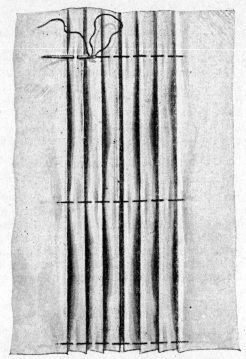

411—Plaits basted for laundering

To Wash Plaited Garments

These can be laundered nicely if a thread is run across the plaits before laundering. Put a thread near the lower edge and at intervals of about six inches above. This holds the plaits while laundering and makes them easy to press. (Illustration 411.)

To Wash Circular Flares

We do not strongly recommend circular styles for wash materials, but some people insist upon using them. To get the best results in washing these styles, be careful to iron on the straight grain of the material, smoothing the lengthwise and crosswise threads into their natural position—never iron on the bias. Hang the garment up for two or three days and the circular parts will sag into the shape they took when the dress was first made.

To Wash Corduroy

Make suds of lukewarm water, and any soap flakes not strong with lye. Move the corduroy up and down in it, rubbing any spots gently with the hands. Rinse thoroughly in clear lukewarm water and lightly squeeze as much moisture as possible out with the hands. Never rub on a board or pass through a wringer, as this injures the nap. Hang in the air until dry, or when almost dry lay face down on a Turkish towel or soft pressing pad and press lightly; be careful to press with the nap.

To Wash Ratine or Turkish Toweling

Make a suds and move the material up and down in it. Do not rub, but just squeeze it. The dirt will drop out, as the weave is open. Rinse thoroughly. Squeeze out as much water as possible with your hands. Never wring it. Hang it up in the air and let it dry. In pressing, thoroughly dampen this material and while it is damp pull out all of the wrinkles. Press lightly on a padded board with a cloth over the material until thoroughly dry. Then brush it thoroughly with a whisk broom, being careful not to pull it.

To Prevent Mildew

Do not allow damp clothes to be left around for any length of time, particularly in warm humid weather. Mildew is almost certain to result. If clothes become mildewed, dampen and rub powdered perborate of soda into the spots, allow to stand a while, then put into boiling water. This applies only to white cottons.

To Wash Silk Hosiery

Silk hosiery should be washed in lukewarm soapy water. Soap should not be rubbed directly on the fabric and hot water must not be used. A mild, neutral soap is best. Do not dry in the sun or in a strong light.   If these directions are followed, stockings will give good service.

Open the stockings by slipping the hands down the inside on both sides of the seam and hang up by the toes so that the water can run out of the top and prevent rotting.

To Wash Woolens

Such as Sweaters or Fabrics Containing Wool

Wool is an extremely sensitive fiber to wash and every possible precaution must be taken to prevent injury or damage to it.   Use the same soap flakes as for thin crêpes, being very careful to follow the directions given with the soap flakes for washing woolens. Squeeze suds through fabric.   Do not rub, as fine woolen fabrics may be easily damaged by too vigorous manipulation during washing.   Rubbing causes the fibers to felt.   Rinse several times in clear lukewarm water.   Squeeze—do not twist.   Dry in the shade. Sometimes more satisfactory results are obtained if woolen fabrics are pressed under a damp cloth.   Sweaters, etc., may be measured before washing, stretched to proper dimensions and laid flat on a soft cloth until dry.

Some woolen yarns are not washable on account of an inherent tendency to felt and shrink.   It is not possible to predict which wools will or will not shrink.   The best safeguard is to follow the directions printed in this chapter.

Chapter XXXI

REMODELING

Materials—Dyeing—Cleaning—Remodeling Dresses—Coats—Suits—Little Girls' Clothes—Boys' Clothes

AT THE beginning of every season when you are planning your clothes look over your wardrobe and decide what you have that is work remaking and will fill some definite place in your outfit. Do not make over any clothes simply because you have them. If you are not going to need them for the present, brush them thoroughly and put them away carefully until you want them.

Things that are genuinely worn out should be thrown away or given to some charitable institution which can find a use for such materials. Do not try to make them over, for they are not worth the time and effort.

Uses for Various Materials

Materials—Wool materials that are too shabby to be made over can often be used for interlining Winter coats and jackets.

Wool materials and some silks that are shabby on the outside but comparatively fresh on the inside can be turned if the wrong side is nice looking. It may not be exactly like the right side, but if it is presentable it can be used—crêpe satin, for example. Satin, plush, velvet and silks that have a design on one side only can not be turned, for the wrong side is not wearable.

Plush and velvet can be steamed to freshen them, remove the wrinkles and raise the nap. Silks and satins can be steamed to remove bad wrinkles.

Small pieces of material can often be combined to make hats for children, or, if suitable, used for collar and cuff facings.

When combinations of materials are in fashion, remaking is a simple matter. Wool materials can often be combined with satin, taffeta, foulard, or with plaid, striped or checked silk or wool materials. Silks, satins, plushes and velvets can be used with Georgette crêpe, chiffon, silk voile, lace or tulle. Plush and velvet can also be combined with silk and satin. Gingham can be used with chambray, and the heavy cotton and linen materials with batiste, handkerchief linen, etc. In Summer materials one can usually combine white with a color, or a plain color with plaid, checked, striped or figured material.

If one feels inclined to take a little trouble, one can completely disguise a last year's suit or dress by changing it to another color.

Dyeing

Dyeing is a very simple thing, but there are certain hard-and-fast rules in regard to it that must not be disregarded. In the first place, you can not dye a silk or wool material with a dye intended only for cotton and linen. Neither can you dye cotton and linen with a silk and wool dye. In the second place, the material must be prepared carefully for the dyeing. If there are any grease spots or stains they should be removed as thoroughly as possible.

Afterward the material should be washed for two reasons. The first is that if the material is put into the dye soiled, the dirt will mingle with the dye and the result will be muddy instead of bright and clear. The second is that as much of the old dye as possible should be taken out or "discharged," as it is called. Otherwise it will be impossible to predict how the mixture of the two dyes will turn out.

Cottons and linen can be washed in soap and boiling water. Boil the materials about half an hour, changing the water as it becomes discolored. Keep up the washing until the water remains clear—a sure sign that all the dye has been discharged that is likely to do any harm.

Wools and silks can be washed in not too hot soapy water. Do not boil these materials because it rots them. All soap must of course be rinsed out before the material is put into the dye.

It is best to dye the material while it is still wet from the washing as it absorbs the dye more readily and more evenly in that condition. Be sure to follow the directions given with the dye you use. A good reliable dye compound will be accompanied by explicit directions, which you must take care to follow. You must be especially careful in picking out a dye that will suit your material. White, of course, can be dyed any color. Pale shades can be dyed darker or changed into other slightly deeper colors. A material of one color dyed with a dye of a second color will emerge from the fray an entirely different shade from either. For instance, if you dye a yellow material with a light-blue dye, you will get green; while the same light blue over light red makes purple, and over light green makes peacock. A dark-blue dye over brown makes navy blue, and over yellow, bottle green. A brown over blue makes dark brown; over green makes olive brown; over red makes seal brown. There are dozens of combinations and variations of colors that one can bring out by a clever combination of dye and material. One should go back to the old safeguard of experimenting first and doing the actual business afterward.

After you have dyed your material, follow the directions that accompany the dye you are using for rinsing and drying.

Cleaning

If you do not dye your material, clean it carefully. Directions for removing spots, stains, etc., are given on pages 243-246.

Remodeling

Before remodeling look over DELINEATOR and the latest editions of BUTTERICK FASHIONS and consider your dress from the standpoint of the new styles. See exactly what it will need to bring it up to date. It must have the right sleeve and collar and the skirt must be the correct width and length. The waistline must come at the right place. Don't wear a high, Empire waistline when a low or normal waistline is the vogue. Don't wear a belt that gives you a pinched-in waist when a wide waist is in fashion.

Be sure that the collar is not only the right size and shape but is absolutely fresh. Collars get hard wear and a collar that is still good style might be worn and shabby. It should be replaced. The same thing is true of chemisettes, undersleeves, cuffs, etc.

If the dress is to be entirely remodeled, rip it apart with a sharp knife or pointed scissors. Do not stretch the material, especially at the neck and armholes. Brush the seams carefully, and remove all clipped threads. If the material has changed color, use it on the reverse side if possible, even if the weave is slightly different.

It should be cleaned if necessary and thoroughly pressed so that it can be cut exactly as if it were a new material.

After the material has been thoroughly freshened—washed, pressed or dyed—lay it out on the new pattern and see if it requires piecing. If piecing is necessary, make the seams fall in places where they do not show or where they can be covered with trimming.

Coats and Suits

Coats should be remodeled by an up-to-date pattern. If they require piecing, try to let it come at a seam and cover it with a stitched or braided band.

Coats of fur fabrics that have become shabby can often be cut down into coatees when they are in fashion, or into children's coats. When they are too badly worn to remake in that way, there are often unworn portions that can be used for neck pieces and muffs, or for collar and cuff facings for a coat or suit.

Suits are apt to wear out in the skirt first. In a suit of a plain colored wool, silk or linen, a new skirt can often be used, made of the same material in a plaid, check or stripe. If the suit material harmonizes with the jacket, you will have a very smart-looking costume. The great French dressmakers frequently make new suits in combinations of this kind. Sometimes the skirt material is used for collar and cuff facings on the coat.

Little Girls' Clothes

Quite frequently it is easier to cut down a coat suit for one of the children than to remodel it for the mother. But do not use a material that is old and somber for a child without relieving it by a trimming that is bright and youthful-looking. A black-and-white pin-checked wool or a dark serge is apt to make a dull frock for a little girl, but if it is trimmed with bands of contrasting material in a suitable color it becomes childish-looking and pretty.

Children grow so fast that the problem of remaking generally includes lengthening and enlarging.

One-piece dresses can often be lengthened by dropping them from a yoke which gives them new width in the shoulders and also gives them new sleeves.

Skirts can be pieced under tucks, folds, bands, flounces, etc. They can also be dropped from an Empire waistline to a normal waistline or they can be lengthened by a band at the bottom. When middy blouses are worn over a skirt, the skirt can be pieced at the top to lengthen it. The blouse will hide the piecing.

Frequently children's dresses can be made into jumper styles. New blouses will give new sleeves and new width through the body.

Boys' Clothes

In making over half-worn garments into presentable and at the same time durable clothes for boys, such as suits, reefers and overcoats, a tailored finish is the first requirement. It means neat work, even stitching and careful pressing. For the pressing you will need heavy irons, evenly heated, and a piece of unbleached muslin that can be dampened and laid over your work.

In ripping apart the old coat or suit that is to be remodeled for your little son, notice carefully all the small devices of interlining, canvas and stitching that the tailor used in making the garment. You can repeat many of them in your own work.